# WORD
# SPIRIT
# POWER

# WORD
# SPIRIT
# POWER

*The Secret to Empowered Living*

## R. T. KENDALL
## CHARLES CARRIN
## JACK TAYLOR

**Chosen**

a division of Baker Publishing Group
Minneapolis, Minnesota

Published by Chosen Books
11400 Hampshire Avenue South
Bloomington, Minnesota 55438
www.chosenbooks.com

Chosen Books is a division of
Baker Publishing Group, Grand Rapids, Michigan

Printed in the United States of America

Library of Congress Cataloging-in-Publication Data
Kendall, R. T.
    Word spirit power : what happens when you seek all God has to offer /
R.T. Kendall, Charles Carrin, Jack Taylor.
        p.   cm.
    ISBN 978-0-8007-9526-9 (pbk. : alk. paper)
    1. Power (Christian theology). 2. Christian life. 3. Holy Spirit. 4. Bible—
Study and teaching. I. Carrin, Charles. II. Taylor, Jack R. III. Title. IV. Title:
Word spirit power.
BT738.25.K46 2012
248.4—dc23                                                    2012002138

Cover design by Kirk DouPounce, DogEared Design

12   13   14   15   16   17   18        7   6   5   4   3   2   1

# Contents

# Introduction

R. T. Kendall

O n the day I finished writing my part of this book, a friend happened to ask me, "What do you think is missing most in the Church today?" I replied: "Power."

I believe that, generally speaking, for too long the Church has existed with a form of godliness but without power (2 Timothy 3:5). What was promised by Jesus to the earliest Church—namely, power (Luke 24:49; Acts 1:8)—is precisely what we do not have at the present time. It has been stated by more than one observer that if the Holy Spirit were completely withdrawn from the Church today, 90 percent of the work of the Church would carry on as if nothing had happened. Not long ago, a Chinese pastor was given a tour of American evangelical churches. At the end of the tour he was asked, "What is your opinion of American churches?" He replied: "I am amazed at what you accomplish without God."

It is our view as coauthors that, in general, a silent divorce exists in the Church today between the Word and the Spirit. When there is a divorce in a family sometimes the children stay with the father, sometimes with the mother. In this divorce we have what might be labeled "Word" churches and those that could be called "Spirit" churches. Although Jack, Charles and I are not necessarily calling for such churches to come together, we *are* calling for a remarriage between the Word and the Spirit in the Church.

I first met Jack Taylor in July 1985 at the First Baptist Church in Fort Lauderdale, Florida, when Dr. O. S. Hawkins was the senior pastor. Meeting Jack was one of the most humbling experiences of my life. Dr. Hawkins announced that Jack and I would have a book signing on the following Saturday morning. As soon as people got in line to get their book, I noticed that dozens were queuing up for Jack's book. Not a single soul came to get mine, although one or two (feeling sorry for me) finally walked over and purchased my book.

I met Charles Carrin at the Central Baptist Church in Hixon, Tennessee, in the spring of 2000. I was deeply impressed with his preaching and ministry. I felt he should come to Westminster Chapel in London, where I was pastor. He came the following November—and he moved us out of our comfort zone. During that time I remember announcing, "Westminster Chapel is now a Spirit church as well as a Word church." It was pivotal for us and I felt grateful to God that He used Charles as He did.

The next time Jack and I met was at the First Baptist Church in Ada, Oklahoma, in July 2000. Jack and I were invited there to do a "Word and Spirit" conference one weekend. Both of us stayed in the home of our friends Pete and Melissa Cantrell. On the last morning, just before breakfast, Jack walked into the living room where I was talking with Pete and said, "R. T., I'm going to make you rich and famous." This made me laugh. But Jack had reckoned we could work together doing "Word and Spirit" conferences once I retired and moved back from London to the United States.

I liked the idea but wondered: Could we bring Charles along with us? Yes, Jack was all for that. Indeed, the three of us held a memorable "Word Spirit Power" conference in Westminster

Chapel during my final year there. I spent exactly 25 years at Westminster Chapel, retiring in 2002.

Although Jack has made me neither rich nor famous, the three of us have held over fifty "Word Spirit Power" conferences all over America, from Florida to Alaska and from New England to the Southwest. Not all churches apparently want us. We seem to appeal mostly to those who equally want both the preaching of the Word and manifestations of the Holy Spirit. I wish there was not the polarization that exists between the Word and Spirit in churches today. Some may doubt or deny that this polarization exists. You decide as you read our book.

Here's the deal: I am the "Word" man, Jack is the "Spirit" man and Charles is the "Power" man, although the three of us equally believe in these three essentials; we are merely drawing upon our individual gifts. We work beautifully with each other and I thank God for our friendship and our ministry together. Never in my life have I known men for whom respect and appreciation has deepened and grown so much as with them. Each of us will begin our sections in this book with our personal testimonies, then we will speak through these printed pages much as we do when we hold conferences. The only thing missing in this book will be the laying on of hands of conference participants, which is a vital part of our ministry.

We were recently approached by Chosen Books to do a book together. The truth is, we had thought of it—but the invitation has galvanized us. The three of us are over 235 years old, and we have been in the ministry for approximately 170 years! Charles is the oldest, Jack is the best looking and I am the most unworthy and possibly the most grateful. Could it be that our legacy will be this very book rather than in the individual areas where we have sought to leave a deposit?

This book you hold in your hands explains the rationale for our ministry, but—more than that—it is intended to make a contribution to the Church at the present time. We believe in this formula: Word + Spirit = Power. Jesus promised that we would receive "power" (Acts 1:8), but this power is manifested today where the Word is faithfully preached *and* the Holy Spirit is warmly welcomed. Agree or disagree with our premise, I pray that this book will stir you and be a blessing to you but, most of all, that it will bring honor and glory to God.

R. T. Kendall

# PART ONE
# WORD

R. T. KENDALL

# one

# My Testimony:
# "He Can Have It"

But as for you, continue in what you have learned and have become convinced of, because you know those from whom you learned it, and how from infancy you have known the Holy Scriptures, which are able to make you wise for salvation through faith in Christ Jesus. All Scripture is God-breathed and is useful for teaching, rebuking, correcting and training in righteousness, so that the servant of God may be thoroughly equipped for every good work.

2 Timothy 3:14–17

Honor the blood, and honor the Holy Ghost.

R. T. Williams (1883–1946)

This chapter is all about the aspects of my spiritual and theological development that eventually led to this book. I am passing over countless autobiographical events that, though important to me, do not bear directly on the theme of this book. I merely want to show what brought me to the place that I became convinced of the need for the Word and Spirit to come together simultaneously.

I was converted at the age of six on April 5, 1942—which happened to be Easter Sunday. I went to my parents in tears, saying, "I want to be a Christian." My dad had the presence of mind not to wait until we got to church but had me kneel at their bedside right then. I confessed my sins and asked Jesus to come into my heart as Lord and Savior. The only sins I can recall were my speaking rudely to my parents, but in any case I knew I needed to be saved.

I was brought up by godly parents in the Church of the Nazarene in Ashland, Kentucky. It was a lively church; the neighbors called us "Noisy-renes." I reckon we were the tail end of the powerful momentum started in the previous century known as the Cane Ridge Revival, sometimes called America's "Second Great Awakening." We had good preachers who would come to hold "revivals." I was made to go to church every time the door was opened. I hated it then, but not now.

My parents were very strict in their standards. I was not allowed to go to movies or dances. Only reluctantly did my dad eventually allow a TV to come into our home. However, rather than rebel I—for some reason—developed my own private prayer life and became interested in things theological. As a teenager, I prayed fifteen minutes every morning before going to school and another fifteen minutes each evening before going to bed. I read doctrinal books, both regarding soteriology (things pertaining to salvation) and eschatology (doctrine of last things).

When I was 17, on April 8, 1953—during my final year in high school—my mother died. She was only 43. It was a trauma from which I have not fully recovered. I had a two-year-old sister and it was a very difficult time for my father. About a year later he remarried.

## My Call to Preach

In September 1953, I entered Trevecca Nazarene University in Nashville, Tennessee. At the time, I had no specific plans for life except I thought I might want to be a trial lawyer. Then, in the autumn of 1954, owing to the profound influence of a Scottish minister, Dr. John S. Logan, I saw clearly that God was calling me to preach. I never looked back nor doubted this call as being from the Lord since.

I preached my first sermon at the Calvary Church of the Nazarene in Nashville a week later. This happened because I told of my call to preach to a friend as I walked on the Trevecca campus. Rev. M. E. Redford, who was a teacher at Trevecca, overheard the conversation and said to me, "You will preach your first sermon this Wednesday night in my church."

I had two days to prepare my first sermon. My subject was "The Faithfulness of God," based upon Lamentations 3:23, "Great is thy faithfulness" (KJV). My sermon lasted eighteen minutes. Four months later, at age nineteen, I was called to be the pastor of the Church of the Nazarene in Palmer, Tennessee. I remained a student at Trevecca. During the week I attended classes and each Friday afternoon I drove about 115 miles to Palmer, usually returning to Nashville on Sunday evenings.

## My "Damascus Road" Experience

On one occasion, however, I returned to Trevecca on a Monday morning. The date was October 31, 1955. Whereas I would usually play the radio during the entire drive back, on this occasion I felt a deep need to pray instead and turned the radio off.

I remember it as if it were yesterday. It was 6:30 A.M. I was coming to the bottom of Monteagle Mountain on old U.S. Highway 41. As I prayed, a heavy burden came on me, a culmination of an anxiety I had been experiencing for several days. I began to doubt whether I was saved—or "sanctified wholly" (given the theological mindset I had at that time).

In agony I cried out, "Lord, what is going on? Am I not sanctified? Am I not even saved?" Two verses came to my mind: 1 Peter 5:7 ("casting all your care upon him; for he careth for

15

you," KJV) and Matthew 11:30 ("my yoke is easy and my burden is light"). My burden that day was heavy. I began in agony to pray for help to cast all my care upon God, so that I could then say my yoke was easy and my burden light.

Suddenly on my right—as I continued to drive toward Nashville—there was Jesus. I did not see His face, but I knew it was He, praying for me. I never felt such love in my whole life. I could see that He cared more about me than I did myself. I burst into tears as I drove. From that point on I was merely a passive spectator. There was Jesus interceding at God's right hand for me as if putting His relationship with the Father on the line for me. I could not hear what He was saying—I only knew that He was *praying*. But it was clear that He was on my side with an amazing love.

The next thing I remember was about an hour later as I came past the town of Smyrna. I heard Jesus clearly say to the Father, referring to me: "He wants it." The Father replied: "He can have it." At that precise moment, I felt a warm surge go right into my chest. It was not only spiritual but physical—I *felt* it. I immediately thought of John Wesley's heartwarming experience at Aldersgate in London. Wesley wrote in his journal that he felt his heart "strangely warmed." I could say the very same thing.

But there is more. For a brief moment—I would say it was less than a minute—I was allowed to see the face of Jesus. He was looking tenderly at me—with "languid eyes," as John Newton put it in one of his hymns. I call this my "Damascus Road" experience, though it was not exactly like Paul's. It was not my conversion but rather the moment that made the person of Jesus more real to me than anyone around me—*and* gave me an infallible assurance of my salvation.

### How My Theology Began to Change

I arrived at Trevecca about 7:50 A.M. I quickly shaved, walked across the campus and went to my first class—pondering and wondering what all this meant. What in fact happened to me? Was I now sanctified? Was this a "third" work of grace? I knew one thing for sure: I was *saved*. I was *eternally* saved. This was the most amazing thing.

Later in the day an old friend, Wilmer Kerns, came to see me. He asked, "What has happened to you?" I was interested that he asked a question like that. I replied, "Well, something *has* happened to me, although I am not sure what." I only knew one thing: I was eternally saved.

I knew beyond any doubt that I would go to heaven when I die—no matter what may happen in between. It was as though I had actually been to heaven. I had one foot in there, it seemed! Nothing would keep me from being there permanently one day. There are no words to describe how clear this was to me. I knew I could not lose my salvation. My friends said to me, "You will change your opinion on this." I knew I would not—and I have not. That was over 55 years ago.

Other truths were brought home to me as clearly as my salvation. The first I will mention was the absolute reality of the bodily resurrection of Jesus. This witness was so strong that if I had been present at the empty tomb on Easter morning, the awareness of Jesus' resurrection would not have been more real. Second, Jesus' intercession at the right hand of the Father was made real as I drove in the car. This memory would have a long-term influence on me, including my theology, down the road, especially when I would do research at Oxford years later. But yet another truth that was equally clear was the Second Coming of Jesus. I knew with infallible assurance that the person of Jesus would literally return one day—indeed, His Second Coming was as real as His resurrection.

In the succeeding weeks I began to have visions. I once counted about a dozen visions that came unexpectedly to me over the next year. Two of them indicated whom certain friends of mine would marry! These visions were perfectly fulfilled. At least one of them indicated I would have a ministry that would reach around the world.

There is yet still more. I began to see things in the Bible I had not seen before, in addition to the knowledge that I could not lose my salvation. I will mention two of these truths: (1) a sense of sin, and (2) predestination and the sovereign work of the Holy Spirit. You must understand that these truths had been totally and utterly alien to me. If anything, I was taught—almost brainwashed—the opposite.

For one thing, we Nazarenes did not sin. Don't laugh—that is what we were taught. After my experience, however, 1 John 1:8 was brought home to me: "If we say that we have no sin" (KJV) we are deceived. I was thankfully now aware of sin. How I praise God for this revelation of my sinfulness. It may not seem a great revelation to anybody else, but it was to me.

As for predestination, this thought, too, had been so far off my radar screen that I continue to marvel such a truth ever got inside me—but it did. I saw that I was chosen from eternity. The truths of election and predestination were in my heart without my reading the first book on Reformed theology. The nearest I came to these ideas was hearing teaching and preaching against it! I cannot express how amazed I am to this very moment that God would show me such knowledge. I am a grateful, unworthy servant.

In 1956, I was invited to be the assistant to Dr. William Greathouse, then dean of religion at Trevecca. He later became president of Trevecca and eventually general superintendent of the Church of the Nazarene. When I shared my thoughts on predestination, he said, "R. T., you are going off into Calvinism." So? "Well, we don't believe that," he said.

I replied, "Then we are wrong!" I quoted to him verses such as Romans 9:15, "I will have mercy on whom I will have mercy," and that salvation depended on God's mercy (verse 16, KJV). I asked him to explain. He replied: "Give me some time on that." That was 55 years ago.

I should add that Dr. Greathouse and I have remained friends over the years—close friends. In fact, he recommended to Dr.

Dan Boone, now president of Trevecca, that I be given a doctor of divinity degree. The school graciously conferred the D.D. on me in April 2008.

## More Manifestations

What I would later come to see as the immediate and direct witness of the Holy Spirit emerged at various times while I was still at Trevecca. In February 1956, while driving in my car with some friends, I felt a new stirring in my heart. More accurately, I felt it in my stomach. It was as though something was inside me—very deep—that wanted to come out like a well trying to spew out water.

As it began to come up, I began to utter unintelligible sounds. I was embarrassed. I was sure the person next to me heard it. Had I been alone it might have gone on and on, but feeling a little embarrassed I did not let it continue. It lasted only a few seconds. No one said a word, however—to this day!—but I knew I had spoken in tongues. I kept quiet about this for many years, telling only my father (who was surprised to hear such a thing—Nazarenes have a long history of being against "tongues") and Dr. Martyn Lloyd-Jones (who affirmed the experience as genuine).

Yet another thing happened as I drove. It came within seconds of that experience of tongues. I was literally told by the Holy Spirit to resign the Palmer pastorate on the following "May 6" and let the final day be on "May 20." This was as clear to me as if the voice had spoken audibly.

All manifestations of the Spirit need to be checked and verified, so the first thing I did was to confirm by the calendar that both dates were Sundays. Surprise, surprise, they were. Why I was told to resign is not clear, but I obeyed. This was the first occasion of the Holy Spirit speaking directly to me. It happened again in April—when the Spirit told me to turn to Philippians 1:12, a word that kept me consoled for many, many years when I did not understand things that were happening around me.

19

During the summer of 1956, a number of significant things took place in my life. The first was that my grandmother—who had bought me a new Chevrolet to use for my trips to Palmer— took the car back! This was not because I gave up the church in Palmer but because it became obvious my future would not be in my old denomination. I have never blamed her for this. She did what she believed was right for me. It did hurt a bit, however, when she gave the car to my dad—who immediately traded it in on a brand new Chrysler!

In August 1956, I sought out the friendship of Rev. Henry T. Mahan, pastor of the Thirteenth Street Baptist Church of Ashland, Kentucky. This was because I had heard him on the radio and felt that what he was preaching was what had been revealed to me. I found his home address and knocked on his door to ask if I could talk with him. "I think that what you preach is what I believe," I said to him.

He summarized what he taught, assuming I would be put off. He was startled that a Nazarene believed what he was teaching: Calvinism. After that, I listened to Henry Mahan preach the Gospel for many, many months. Although he was not sure what to think of my experience of October 31, 1955, and though I found the services at Thirteenth Street rather cold and dry when compared to what I was used to, I learned a lot in those days. I will be eternally grateful to Henry for the theological foundation and superstructure he helped build for me. What had been revealed to me by the Bible and the Holy Spirit (without my reading a single book on Calvinism) was enlarged upon by Henry's teaching. I was eventually ordained by the Thirteenth Street Baptist Church.

My dad was convinced I had "broken with God" or else I would have had fruit to show I was in the Lord's will. I had no church in which to preach. No one believed in me. Trying to make him feel better, I thought about certain visions God had given me, including an international ministry. I foolishly tried to convince him by sharing one of those visions. "When will this be fulfilled?" he understandably asked. I answered, "One year from now." He asked me to sign a statement to that effect, which I did. But one year later, I was not even in the ministry at all.

## The Move to England

While my theology was being honed in those years (1956–57), I was in an ecclesiastical wilderness. I had no credible future at the time. I worked as a salesman to pay my bills.

After becoming the pastor of the Lauderdale Manors Baptist Church in Fort Lauderdale (1968–1970), I entered Southern Baptist Theological Seminary in Louisville, Kentucky. In 1973, my family and I went to England for me to work toward the D.Phil. degree at Oxford. During the years 1973 to 1976, my relationship with Dr. Martyn Lloyd-Jones became a significant ingredient regarding my theological development and also my immediate future: He helped to refine my doctrinal understanding even further and ended up putting me in Westminster Chapel. I was the minister there, as mentioned, for exactly 25 years—from 1977 to 2002.

In those days at Oxford, when Dr. and Mrs. Lloyd-Jones would come to visit us, he would repeatedly say to me, "Never forget your Nazarene background. That is what has saved you." I was surprised to learn he knew a lot about Nazarenes, feeling they once had authentic power that was sadly lacking among Reformed ministers and churches in Britain. When I accepted the pastorate at Westminster he said to me, "Preach like a Nazarene." He felt that so many of the Reformed men were—in his words—"perfectly orthodox, perfectly useless."

Dr. Lloyd-Jones used to say to me, "I am an eighteenth-century man," by which he meant he loved the era of George Whitefield and John Wesley more than the Puritans of the seventeenth century. He regarded himself as a "Calvinistic Methodist." He stressed the *immediate and direct* witness of the

Holy Spirit," that is, the Holy Spirit's *own* witness being the way we know for sure we are saved. So many people have only a soteriological doctrine of the Holy Spirit, meaning the Holy Spirit "applies" the preaching of the Gospel—which of course is absolutely right. But this view takes little account of the Holy Spirit's immediate and direct witness. The absence of this immediate and direct witness, then, is what often paves the way for a ministry that is "perfectly orthodox, perfectly useless."

My preaching ministry at Westminster was almost entirely expository, although our Friday night "School of Theology" dealt with doctrinal themes. For the first five years, my ministry at Westminster was uneventful—except that I had the privilege of sharing my preparation with Dr. Lloyd-Jones for the first four years. It was during those four years he taught me how to think. He died on March 1, 1981.

### Taking Risks

That same year, I accepted the presidency of the Fellowship of Independent Evangelical Churches. At their annual meeting in April 1982, it turned out they were looking for a speaker who could fill Westminster Chapel. I suggested Arthur Blessitt—the man who has carried a cross around the world. They eventually agreed. When Arthur came I was so taken with him that I invited him to preach for us during May. He turned us upside down. You can read about this in my book *In Pursuit of His Glory*—an account of my 25 years at Westminster Chapel.

Owing to Arthur's influence we made some significant changes—changes, I am ashamed to say, I would not have had the courage to carry out had not Arthur shaken us up. There was severe opposition to the changes we began to make, which included (1) giving an invitation for people to respond publicly to my preaching (which Dr. Lloyd-Jones did not do), (2) singing choruses (which as far as I know had never been done) as well as hymns, and (3) witnessing on the streets (our Pilot Light ministry). Most of our members were thrilled with the new era that had begun. A few were unhappy, however, with these changes. Certain deacons even turned the issue into a theological one. That backfired. The church stood with me and against these deacons. But those were extremely hard days—in fact, the hardest of my life.

I later invited Paul Cain—known for his unusual prophetic gift—to preach for us. I have to say with deepest regret that this man greatly disappointed me by his personal failures that became well known after my wife, Louise, and I returned to America. But to leave him out of this book would be to omit important history. One evening—on October 26, 1990—when sitting in a restaurant on Victoria Street, I said to Paul, "You need my theology, I need your power." One might say that this very book was born in that moment. I say this because the notion of Word and Spirit was implanted in my own mind then in a new way and the idea began to grow.

On October 16, 1992, Paul Cain and I held the first "Word and Spirit" conference at Wembley Conference Centre. Lyndon Bowring chaired the meeting and Graham Kendrick wrote a new hymn based on the idea of the Word and Spirit coming together. I would represent the Word aspect and Paul would represent the Spirit aspect, since his ministry had not been theological but mostly with reference to signs and wonders (prophecy and healing). The irony of the day was that although Paul was the one most people came to hear, it was my own messages that became publicized. Paul gave three talks—mostly about the Word—and my own ministry turned out to be prophetic. This was not planned, it just happened that way. My address called "The Post-Charismatic Era" (which I have rewritten slightly to comprise chapter three of this book) got me into more trouble than any talk I have given in over fifty years of ministry. The charismatics did not like it because I compared them to Ishmael. The evangelicals did not like it for other reasons—and their main magazine poked fun at it.

23

In 1994, I endorsed the "Toronto Blessing," as it was called. I first heard of it one evening when Lyndon Bowring, Charlie Colchester (one of the churchwardens at Holy Trinity Church, Brompton) and I were having a Chinese dinner in the Soho area of London. Charlie spoke up, "Have you guys heard about this Toronto thing?" No, we hadn't. He began to describe how the laying on of hands caused people to fall to the floor uncontrollably and start laughing their heads off. I was immediately concerned but also reflective—and yet if you had put me under a lie detector and asked whether I thought this manifestation was of God, I would have passed with flying colors by saying, "No." I even cautioned the members of Westminster Chapel the following Sunday, stating, "This is not it"—meaning, this was not the revival we were praying for.

Sometime later, Ken Costa, the other churchwarden of Holy Trinity, asked if I had any sermons on 1 John 4:1–4. Yes, four, in fact, I told him. I sent them to him and he then asked me to lunch. I went armed to warn him about this Toronto thing, but I came away sobered and convicted that I was in danger of trespassing on something that was holy and sacred. I was truly shaken. I climbed down publicly as fast as I could, urging the people of Westminster to be open to it.

It was a good while before the Toronto Blessing manifestations made their way into Westminster Chapel, but they finally did. We even saw people healed. I invited John Arnott, leader of the Toronto church where the phenomenon took place, to preach for me. Eventually, I also invited Rodney Howard-Browne (an entire chapter is devoted to him in my book *In Pursuit of His Glory*). By this time, I was pretty much "labeled," and there was nothing I could do to change people's perception of me. I found it embarrassing.

The ingredients that led to my present position regarding the Word and Spirit can be summed up: (1) my experience of October 31, 1955, which led me to embrace Reformed theology, (2) my Oxford research, which helped me to clarify certain theological positions, and (3) the influence of Dr. Lloyd-Jones, which encouraged my openness to the direct witness of the Holy Spirit.

## The Decision to Retire

One day in 2000, I was pondering the issue of how long I should stay at Westminster Chapel. I can't say I was praying, only thinking and talking to myself. How long should I stay? "I will stay exactly 25 years," I said to myself. "But what will I do once I retire? I suppose I will become a recluse in the Florida Keys and spend my time fishing, since nobody in America knows me."

At that moment, a voice inside me said, "Your ministry in America will be to charismatics." "Oh no," I responded. "I would prefer to minister to evangelicals. I have the credentials. I know how they think. I have what they need." But, no, I would minister to charismatics.

I am sorry, but this is certainly not what I would have chosen. And yet the Church generally is better off for the charismatic movement. Not only that, but most churches worth their salt in Britain are largely charismatic.

Yet being welcomed by charismatics in the U.S. is exactly the way it turned out. Louise and I moved to Key Largo, Florida, in February 2002. One week later, I held a "Word Spirit Power" conference with Jack Taylor and Charles Carrin. We have traveled since then to many places, sometimes crossing theological and ecclesiastical lines. Here again is the formula we put forth: Word + Spirit = Power. How much good have we done? Who knows?

Sometimes I have wondered if my own ministry has been as welcome in some charismatic churches as Jack's and Charles's. Rightly or wrongly, I have felt that some charismatic churches tolerated me but gladly welcomed Jack and Charles. This has not been true with all churches, however. I have often felt, however, that those churches that were so keen to see signs and wonders did not particularly relish my own contribution.

It may be in any case that this very book will be our lasting legacy. I believe our premise is solid. I believe it is widely needed today. I therefore pray you will read on and that God will make this book a blessing to you. The next chapter is a very slight rewriting of my first address at the aforementioned Wembley Conference Centre.

two

# The Remarriage of the Word and Spirit

Jesus replied, "You are in error because you do not know the Scriptures or the power of God. At the resurrection people will neither marry nor be given in marriage; they will be like the angels in heaven. But about the resurrection of the dead—have you not read what God said to you, 'I am the God of Abraham, the God of Isaac, and the God of Jacob?' He is not the God of the dead but of the living." When the crowds heard this, they were astonished at his teaching.

Matthew 22:29–33

My message and my preaching were not with wise and persuasive words, but with a demonstration of the Spirit's power.

1 Corinthians 2:4

Our gospel came to you not simply with words but also with power, with the Holy Spirit and deep conviction. You know how we lived among you for your sake.

1 Thessalonians 1:5

Following Jesus' eventful encounter with the Sadducees, Matthew reports that the crowds were "astonished" at His teaching (Matthew 22:33). This is the same Greek word—*ekpleesso*—that is used when Jesus finished the Sermon on the Mount: The people were "amazed" at this teaching (Matthew 7:28). It is used when Jesus cast out a demon: "They were all amazed at the greatness of God" (Luke 9:43). It goes to show that Jesus could astonish people with His teaching as well as with a miracle before their eyes. I suspect most of us imagine that only a miracle could amaze people. Jesus, however, could do it with His word as well as with His power.

Graham Kendrick wrote a hymn, "Restore, O Lord, the Honor of Your Name." How do you suppose the restoration of that honor is to come about? Some might say it will come with a demonstration of signs and wonders. That could be true. I take the view, however, that God is generally withholding the phenomena of signs and wonders to the Church of our generation until two things coalesce: the Scriptures and the power of God.

There is more than one way to put this. We could call it the combination of the Word and Spirit. Paul could testify that his Gospel preaching came "not simply" with words but "with the Holy Spirit" (1 Thessalonians 1:5). Indeed, Paul's message and preaching were not "with wise and persuasive words, but with a demonstration of the Spirit's power" (1 Corinthians 2:4). There is yet another way to put this, as we will see below: when the Word and name of God are given their rightful place.

Jesus' way of putting this across to the Sadducees was to refer to the Scriptures and the power of God. The Greek word for power is *dunamis*—from which we derive the word "dynamite." It is what was promised to the waiting disciples at Pentecost (Luke 24:49; Acts 1:4): "Stay in [Jerusalem] until you have been clothed with power from on high." "But you will receive power when the Holy Spirit comes on you" (Acts 1:8). The coming together of the two—the Scriptures and the power of

God—provides the only explanation for what happened when Peter preached on the Day of Pentecost.

By "Scriptures" I mean the Bible—the Old and New Testaments—which I hold to be infallible. "All Scripture is God-breathed and is useful for teaching, rebuking, correcting and training in righteousness, so that the servant of God may be thoroughly equipped for every good work" (2 Timothy 3:16–17). The writers of Scripture were men who "spoke from God as they were carried along by the Holy Spirit" (2 Peter 1:21).

The Bible is God's final revelation of Christian doctrine. It does not matter a person's maturity, experience or profile in the church: Anyone who claims to have received a "word from God," or who wants to give a prophecy, should be made to come under the objective scrutiny of infallible Scripture. Those who treat prophecies with "contempt" (1 Thessalonians 5:20) not only grieve the Holy Spirit but risk forfeiting a word that could be life-changing. Just as we are commanded to entertain strangers that might be angels (Hebrews 13:2), so we should listen when a person claims to have a word that comes from God. But that word must always be examined in the light of God's infallible Word. To quote Dr. Martyn Lloyd-Jones: "The Bible was not given to us to replace the supernatural or miraculous but to correct abuses."

The power of God is what lies behind the miraculous. It is what can make preaching irresistible, as the apostle Stephen experienced (Acts 6:10). It is a supernatural force that has no natural explanation. So many healings also have a natural explanation, as when medicine or surgery is used. There is certainly nothing wrong in taking appropriate medicine or having an operation. Yet when you pray for the healing of a person who has benefited from medical expertise, you cannot be sure that healing was truly supernatural. It may have a natural explanation. Supernatural, however, means "above" or "beyond" the natural. The raw power of God is capable of healing anybody, including raising one from the dead.

## Both the Scriptures *and* God's Power

Jesus stated that the Sadducees were ignorant of *both* the Scriptures and the power of God (Matthew 22:29). With some believers it is one or the other. There are those who are well acquainted with the Scriptures, knowing their Bibles, their doctrine, their Church history. People like this can smell heresy a mile away. There are those on the other hand who have been acquainted with the raw power of God—experiencing the infilling of the Holy Spirit, demonstrating the gifts of the Spirit, seeing healings and miracles. People like this can smell dead orthodoxy a mile away.

What is wrong with either emphasis? Nothing. Take those in the evangelical or Reformed tradition. They say that we must earnestly contend for the faith once delivered unto the saints, that we must recover our Reformation heritage, that we must return to the God of Jonathan Edwards and Charles Spurgeon, that we must be sound in our doctrine. What is wrong with this message? Nothing. It is absolutely right.

Now take those who come from a Pentecostal or charismatic perspective. They say that we must recover apostolic power, that there must be a renewal of the gifts of the Spirit, that we must get back to the book of Acts in which there were signs and wonders, that what is needed is an undoubted demonstration of the raw, unmediated power of God. What is wrong with this message? Nothing. It is absolutely true as well.

The thesis of this chapter is that the Church generally will struggle on and on in its plea for God to restore the honor of His name until the matter involves not one or the other but both: the simultaneous combination of the Scriptures and the power of God. Here are two things we all ought to know—indeed, two things the Sadducees did not know—which ought to be emphasized and experienced simultaneously.

The Sadducees were largely from priestly families. They traced their ancestry to Zadok. They were the aristocracy of their day. They were fewer in number than the Pharisees but far more influential. What is more, they "knew it all." They were like the saying, "You can always tell a Harvard man but you can't tell him much." They did not merely *think* they were the ultimate experts on the Pentateuch and the Law of Moses but *knew* they were.

The Sadducees had minimal respect for the prophetic gift; their authority was Moses. They regarded Old Testament prophets as second class. Their distinctive doctrinal assumptions were that there was (1) no resurrection of the body (Acts 23:8), (2) no such thing as angels and (3) no such thing as disembodied spirits (they believed that the soul died with the body). They despised Jesus of Nazareth. The fact that the Pharisees felt the same way about Jesus was not enough to win the Sadducees over. The Sadducees were determined to prove two things: that their doctrinal distinctives were correct and that Jesus was to be ignored as a temporal phenomenon that would soon pass.

The Sadducees were very proud of themselves for coming up with an airtight case that would prove their point and put Jesus in His place. The account begins in Matthew 22:23. They came to Jesus with a fictitious story that supposedly vindicated their teaching to the hilt. They pointed out Moses' teaching that if a man dies without having children, his brother must marry the widow and have children for him. "Now there were seven brothers among us. The first one married and died, and since he had no children, he left his wife to his brother. The same thing happened to the second and third brother, right on down to the seventh. Finally, the woman died. Now then, at the resurrection, whose wife will she be of the seven, since all of them were married to her?" (verses 25–28).

Jesus did not respond by saying, "You're making that up." His reply was, "You are in error because you do not know the Scriptures or the power of God" (verse 29). They were in error—indeed, the Greek word *planao* means they were "deceived." "You are 'wrong,'" says Jesus (ESV). What a thing to say to those who think they know it all! Yet, how many of us have the honesty and integrity and objectivity about ourselves to see and admit it if we have been deceived? Surely if any of us has been deceived we want to know about it—as soon as possible! I would rather die than to preach what is not true.

But in the case of the Sadducees their deception and unteachable spirit sprang from *ignorance*. "You do not know." It is rather interesting that the Greek word used here is not *ginosko*—a word that largely refers to what is revealed—but *iodate*, which means the Sadducees were not even acquainted with well-known facts they felt they were experts on! Fancy this: "You are ignorant of the Scriptures," says Jesus.

Is it truly possible that the prestigious and erudite Sadducees were ignorant of Scripture? Yes. Can you imagine talking this way to a seminary professor, an Oxford don or a New Testament scholar—telling them that they are ignorant? Jesus was devoid of any fear or intimidation by these men. He was at home in this dialogue! They were the ones who were becoming intimidated. When you and I are equipped with the right knowledge of God's Word and simultaneously filled with the Holy Spirit, we will not be intimidated by the most learned and powerful people in the world. We, too, will be at home in disputing with them.

### How Well Do You Know Your Bible?

I don't mean to be unfair, but I must ask you, reader: Are you ignorant of God's Word? Are you? How well do you know your Bible? I have a deep-seated fear that the present generation of Christians generally does not know the Bible.

The time was that even if Christians knew little of God's power, at least they knew the Bible. Not only preachers but laymen knew the Bible. In a previous generation a typical church member knew his Bible so well that if you started to quote a verse the person could finish it—and tell you where it is in Scipture! Not so today, sadly.

What about you? Have you read the Bible? Jesus actually put that question to the Sadducees: "Have you not *read* what God said to you?" (verse 31, emphasis mine). So how often do *you* read the Bible? Do you read it daily? Do you have a Bible reading plan? Perhaps you need a plan that will take you through the whole Bible in one year. I urge you, go find a Bible reading plan that will take you through the entire Old and New Testament in a year—and start today.

Jesus said to them, "You are ignorant of the Scriptures"— ignorant of the Pentateuch, the first five books of Moses and the Law. It was an insult to tell Sadducees they did not know their Bible!

Jesus then added, "You are equally ignorant of God's power." "You are in error because you do not know the Scriptures *or* the power of God" (verse 29, emphasis mine). Why bring up this matter of the power of God? The Sadducees were not the slightest bit interested in that subject. What about you? What do *you* personally know about the power of God? Is it second-hand to you—that is, you have only read about it in Scripture or perhaps in Church history?

As for the Sadducees, they had not come to talk about God's power. That was the furthest thing from their minds. It was Jesus who brought up the subject of the power of God. Jesus initiated a matter they had not come to discuss; nothing seemed more irrelevant to them.

I turn to you again, reader: Have you felt that your knowledge of the Bible is enough? Are you among those who feel that an emphasis on sound doctrine is all that really matters, that it is all that matters to God? Are you one of those evangelicals who have thought that talk of God's power being manifested today is nonsense and was meant for the apostolic era only?

I must ask you: What do you do when you come across a demon-possessed person? Are we to believe that demon possession ceased with the apostolic age? Are we to believe that God would leave us stripped of any power to deal with the demonic?

Moreover, the case for "cessationism"—the belief that the miraculous ceased with the closing of the canon of Scripture and that now having the Bible is enough—is the weakest teaching ever to emerge in evangelicalism. Yet, sadly, some good orthodox men and women put all their eggs in this fragile basket. Don't do it!

## A Pharaoh Who Knew Not Joseph

The Church today, speaking generally, is like the Pharaoh who knew not Joseph. I refer to Joseph, the son of Jacob who became prime minister of Egypt and won the favor of the Pharaoh. Joseph brought all his family to Egypt and over time the children of Israel would multiply to many thousands. The Pharaoh whom Joseph knew gave the people of Israel everything they wanted.

That Pharaoh died, however, and there arose a Pharaoh who did not know of the previous Pharaoh's commitment to Joseph and his family. The new Pharaoh was ignorant of that generation. To him, it was as though there never had been a Joseph. He therefore looked at the increasing children of Israel as a threat—and he made them slaves.

A few years ago I was invited to have dinner with the late John Wimber, a gifted teacher and world renowned in the Church. I had been to hear him at Royal Albert Hall and was impressed. On the day I was to have a meal with John, however, I was unexpectedly given a "word" for him. I was not particularly looking forward to the meal by this time, but I went and shared my "word" with him anyway. I looked at him and said, "John, you taught the other night that Luther and Calvin gave us the Word in the sixteenth century but that we are called to do the 'works' in the twentieth century. Is that not what you said?"

"That is exactly what I said," he replied.

"But, John," I continued, "you are teaching this to Pharaohs who don't know Joseph. This is a generation of Pharaohs who feel they owe nothing to and know little of our historic past— and who *don't know their Bible*. You are implying that just

34

because Luther and Calvin gave us a word that people today have that same word. They don't."

As John listened, he put his fingers on his chest and said, "You have touched the very vortex of my thinking at this moment. I accept what you say." I appreciated his spirit. Whether it made any difference with him after that occasion, I don't know.

Why should we know our Bibles so well? For one thing, Jesus said that when the Holy Spirit comes, He would *remind* the disciples of what He had taught them. Christ's disciples had been trained, taught and cared for. They had heard a lot and learned a lot. But what if they forgot what they had heard or learned? Jesus said to them not to worry: "But the Advocate, the Holy Spirit, whom the Father will send in my name, will teach you all things and *will remind you of everything* I have said to you" (John 14:26, emphasis mine).

Here is the wonderful thing: The Holy Spirit will remind us of what we were taught and what we learned. If you ask, "Why go to Bible studies? Why read the Bible every day? Why sit under teaching and the preaching of the Bible, especially if it is boring?" I answer: because the Holy Spirit will bring it back to you when you need it.

I happen to believe that a great—truly great—outpouring of the Spirit is coming just down the road. In the next chapter, I call it "the coming of Isaac." If I get to see it (which I expect to do, at least the beginnings of it), that means it is not far away (I am 75 years old). I also believe, though, that God will use those who have disciplined themselves to read the Bible and have gotten to know God well through it.

Simply put, God will use those in His next great movement who have sought His face more than His hand, who have searched His Word and stood in awe of it. Job could say that he esteemed the words of the mouth of the Lord more than his daily bread (Job 23:12). The psalmist said, "I have hidden your word in my heart that I might not sin against you" (Psalm 119:11). Remember: At a time you least expect, the Holy Spirit will bring to your mind what you took the time to read and learn. I guarantee it.

## The Word and the Name

Another way of framing my thesis here is that the Word of God and the name of God are rejoined. You see, two important ways God has chosen to unveil Himself in the Bible are by His Word and by His name.

The Word is what came to Abraham, Isaac and Jacob. It is the Word that Abraham believed—being persuaded of the sheer *promise* that his seed would be as numerous as the stars in the heavens. What was the result of believing that word? God credited Abraham with righteousness. Abraham became Paul's chief example for his teaching of justification by faith (Genesis 15:6; Romans 4).

Believing the promise is the way people are saved to this very day.

> But what does it say? "The word is near you; it is in your mouth and in your heart," that is, the message concerning faith we proclaim: If you declare with your mouth, "Jesus is Lord," and believe in your heart that God raised him from the dead, you will be saved. For it is with your heart that you believe and are justified, and it is with your mouth that you profess your faith and are saved.
>
> Romans 10:8–10

This is the Gospel: It comes through hearing the Word. The Gospel was first preached to Abraham (Galatians 3:8). The name of God was first disclosed to Moses. God appeared to him at the burning bush, and after telling Moses to take off his shoes, God said to him, "I am the God of your father, the God of Abraham, the God of Isaac and the God of Jacob" (Exodus 3:6). This is the verse Jesus quoted to the Sadducees in Matthew 22:32.

Consider this, however: "God also said to Moses, 'I am the LORD. I appeared to Abraham, to Isaac and to Jacob as God Almighty, but by my name the LORD I did not make myself known to them'" (6:2–3). How could this be? Abraham knew God through His *Word* but did not know His name—so says Exodus 6:3. This was partly because God's Word has priority over His name.

We are saved by hearing the Word. That is how God made Himself known to Abraham. It is how Abraham was *saved;* it is also how you and I are saved. Abraham was arguably the prototype Christian. Scripture says he saw Jesus' day and was glad (John 8:56). As I have stated, Abraham's experience was the foundation of Paul's teaching in Romans and Galatians. That experience, however, was Word-oriented; it was faith in God's Word.

### The Gospel: Rooted in the Word

This explains how it is possible for the Church to continue without signs and wonders. We are not saved by signs and wonders; we are saved by the Gospel—by hearing the Word. The Gospel is complete without signs and wonders. The Bible, however, is not complete without signs and wonders—though the Gospel is. This is why the Billy Grahams of this world have been used to save millions for Christ. Billy Graham does not emphasize signs and wonders; he has preached the Gospel—the Word. This is the way people are saved—always have been, always will be!

Have you ever wondered why the psalmist could say, "For thou hast magnified thy word above all thy name" (Psalm 138:2, KJV)? Most versions gloss over the Hebrew in Psalm 138:2. The English Standard Version, however, quotes the Hebrew literally in a footnote: "You have exalted your word above all your name." Why did David state this as he did? It is because the Word must always have priority over the phenomena of what would be associated with His name. The Word came first. Not only that, God is more concerned about His Word—His honor and integrity—than He is His name, His reputation. He is the most maligned Person in the universe. How often is it asked, "Why does God allow evil and suffering when He could so easily stop it?" God's reputation has suffered and will continue to do so. He will clear His name one day. In the meantime, the Word has priority. The Gospel is the good news that comes through preaching (1 Corinthians 1:21). The Gospel is the way we are saved. This is the main thing.

Yet one day God *appeared* to Moses. Moses got up that day like any other day. He was watching sheep at the foot of Mount Horeb when he saw a bush on fire. Perhaps nothing was unusual about that. I was in Egypt not long ago, at the base of Mount Sinai, or Horeb, and there are bushes all around that could easily catch fire. When bushes are on fire, however, they burn up. Not so with the bush Moses observed; he noticed after a while that the bush did not burn up.

One of two things was true: Either the bush was different or the fire was different. So Moses decided to have a look "and see this strange sight—why the bush does not burn up" (Exodus 3:3). God said, "STOP—don't try to figure it out!" The occasion meant that Moses was never to be the same again. God unveiled His name: "I AM WHO I AM" (3:14).

An unprecedented phenomenon accompanied the unveiling of God's name: signs and wonders. It began with the burning bush. It continued with Aaron's rod turning into a serpent. It continued further with the ten plagues upon Egypt, culminating with the Passover. Then came the Israelites crossing the Red Sea on dry land. After that came the manna in the desert. Through all of these events the revelation of God's name was inaugurated with power—signs and wonders that defied a natural explanation.

How do we summarize the Word and the name? The Word of God pertains to His *integrity*: His precepts and faithful promises, His reliability and trustworthiness, His inability to tell a lie. The

Bible is God's integrity put on the line. Our view of inspiration bears repeating here: "All Scripture is God-breathed and is useful for teaching, rebuking, correcting and training in righteousness" (2 Timothy 3:16). "For prophecy never had its origin in the human will, but prophets, though human, spoke from God as they were carried along by the Holy Spirit" (2 Peter 1:21).

The name of God pertains to His identity but also to His *honor*: His reputation, power, glory and influence. It is what gives Him open vindication before people, when He is pleased to manifest Himself. Moses pleaded with God to forgive Israel for their rebellion, concerned that God's reputation appeared to be at stake. If God destroyed His own people, Moses said, "The Egyptians will hear about it!" (Numbers 14:13). The power of God's name was also invested in Jesus' name. "And his *name*—by faith in his *name*—has made this man strong whom you see and know, and the faith that is through Jesus has given the man this perfect health in the presence of you all" (Acts 3:16, ESV, emphasis mine).

God magnifies His Word above His name in the meantime because His integrity is more important to Him than His reputation. He will always be true to Himself by what He states and promises. He keeps His Word whatever people may say about Him. He can wait for His name to be cleared for another day. He can also reveal the power that comes from Jesus' name whenever He wills. But the Word has priority over the name. You and I should have the same priority. Yet we are to make no mistake about it: The Bible is not completely proclaimed without signs, wonders and miracles. The name of God, from the moment it was revealed to Moses, was accompanied with signs and wonders.

As for the Sadducees, they knew neither the Scriptures *nor* the power of God. Not only that, the very verse Jesus quoted—one they thought they understood backward and forward—had *not* been understood by them! Exodus 3:6 ("I am the God of Abraham, the God of Isaac and the God of Jacob") would have been as familiar to them as John 3:16 is to us. Yet the Sadducees never picked up the real meaning of Exodus 3:6. In fact, you can detect Jesus' sarcasm when He said, "Have you not *read* what God said to you?" (Matthew 22:31, emphasis mine). He is plainly asking them if they have read one of the most quoted verses in the Old Testament! He is going to show them that they have not understood this verse, either.

Jesus then raises with them the most obvious issue: *Whatever happened to these very men*—Abraham, Isaac and Jacob? Were they just relics of the past? Did they die like dogs or cattle or trees? Where are they today? Jesus then gave the Sadducees the shock of their lives. He not only turned their smug theological assumption on its head, but in doing so He affirmed the resurrection of the dead, angels and the immortality of souls. He said to them, "At the resurrection people will neither marry nor be given in marriage; they will be like the angels in heaven" (verse 30). Resurrection meant the end of death. There would be no need for procreation of the race, for we will be like angels in heaven.

Then came His final word, as if it were a P.S.: "He is not the God of the dead but of the living" (verse 32). In a word: Abraham, Isaac and Jacob are alive and well—in heaven right now with the angels! Their souls are with God, their disembodied spirits are with Him, and they are at this precise moment worshiping Him. No wonder, then, that the crowds were "astonished" at Jesus' teaching. He could astonish people by what He *taught* as well as by what He *did*.

The fact that the crowds were astonished at Jesus' answer is a dead giveaway that the Sadducees were left speechless. They were stunned by what Jesus said, and it showed on their faces, which the people could see. There was nothing left for them to say—which added to the amazement of the crowds.

## The Basis for True Power

Contained in Matthew 22:29, then, is the basis for true power. As we have observed, Jesus promised *power* to those who tarried in Jerusalem (Luke 24:49). He promised power after the Spirit of God came down on the disciples. Paul warned of having a form of godliness but denying its power (2 Timothy 3:5).

What is the basis for this power? First, it begins with the reading of the Scriptures. "Have you not read . . . ?" (Matthew 22:31). I raise the question again to you, reader: How much do you read the Bible? How well do you know the Bible? As I have stated, we all need a Bible reading plan that will keep us in the Word every single day.

Second, power comes with the revelation of the Scriptures. "What God said to you" (verse 31). This was Jesus' stinging word for the Sadducees—that smug, cynical, sure and sad lot of men. God had said it to Moses, and then Jesus said to them: "This word is for you." That also means it is for us! It means personal revelation. When God grips you—the Spirit applying the Word like a laser beam—then you know you have not been deceived.

Third, power can be found in a rethinking of the Scriptures, which we think we know so well. It was almost an insult to the Sadducees when Jesus suggested they had not even *read* Exodus 3:6. In any case, these learned men missed the obvious meaning of it altogether. They thought they knew everything implied in Exodus 3:6, for it had been the ABCs to them. To them it meant only that they worship the same God in their day as the patriarchs worshiped in their own day. "You've missed the real meaning," says Jesus to them. His point: It means Abraham, Isaac and Jacob are *alive*. Our God is not the God of the dead but of the living!

I wonder how many of us are locked in to a point of view of certain Bible verses we think we know so well, when in truth we have not scratched the surface of them. Many of us have uncritically accepted a point of view—a "hand-me-down" understanding of oft-quoted verses with no personal revelation. That is not to mention acquiring the real meaning of a verse.

Fourth, there is a need for the release of the Spirit. Where does that come from? It comes from the Holy Spirit Himself. In order to know and understand the meaning of Scriptures, we must get on good terms with the Author, the Holy Spirit. To be on good terms with the Holy Spirit means we must not grieve Him by bitterness (Ephesians 4:30–31) or quench Him by disavowing what He may want to do in our church, not to mention in our lives (1 Thessalonians 5:19).

It is one thing to have an orthodox doctrine of the Holy Spirit or the Trinity. It is another thing to be sensitive to the Third Person of the Godhead. We must all realize that unforgiveness and holding grudges grieves the Spirit—which is often what keeps us from understanding Scripture! This means you and I must not only affirm the Gospel but obey the Word in our personal lives; there are no shortcuts. This release of the Spirit, moreover, will not always come by standing in a line merely to get the laying on of hands. The Holy Spirit wrote the Bible—it is infallible, the Spirit's greatest product. When we are gripped by the Word, however, and we take care to honor the Holy Spirit, there will be a renewal of power—and with it, I believe, the restoration of the honor of God's name.

You may say: "If I could have Jesus Himself giving me the exposition and interpretation of Scripture, I, too, would be astonished, as the crowds were when Christ outpointed the Sadducees." I reply: You have the greatest expositor with you—the Holy Spirit—and He will be released to the degree that you esteem and magnify and also obey His Word. If God magnifies His Word above His name, should we not also?

I was named after my dad's favorite preacher, Dr. R. T. Williams, who used to say to young people entering the ministry: "Honor the blood, and honor the Holy Ghost." This means focusing upon the Gospel and being unashamed of the blood of Christ—but also being open to the immediate and direct witness and work of the Holy Spirit. The Holy Spirit may have surprising plans for us!

## The Silent Divorce

A silent divorce has taken place in the Church, generally speaking, between the Word and the Spirit. And when there is a divorce, sometimes the children stay with the mother, sometimes with the father. In this divorce, we have those on the "Word" side and those on the "Spirit" side. Those who go to "Word" churches do not expect to *see* much; they go to hear. "Thank you for your word," is a typical comment to the preacher following the sermon. When people go to "Spirit" churches, they usually do not expect to *hear* much; they go to see.

But when the two are brought together, the simultaneous combination will mean spontaneous combustion. The day will come—and I believe it is at hand—when, as my friend Lyndon Bowring put it, those who come to see will hear and those who come to hear will see.

# three

# Isaac Is Coming!

Abraham fell facedown; he laughed and said to himself, "Will a son be born to a man a hundred years old? Will Sarah bear a child at the age of ninety?" And Abraham said to God, "If only Ishmael might live under your blessing!" Then God said, "Yes, but your wife Sarah will bear you a son, and you will call him Isaac. I will establish my covenant with him. . . . And as for Ishmael, I have heard you: I will surely bless him . . . and I will make him into a great nation. But my covenant I will establish with Isaac."

Genesis 17:17–21

During the next few decades there will be two distinct moves of the Holy Spirit across the Church in Great Britain. The first move will affect every church that is open to receive it and will be characterized by a restoration of the baptism and gifts of the Holy Spirit. The second move of the Holy Spirit will result in people leaving historic churches and planting new churches. In the duration of each of these moves, the people who are involved will say, "This is the great revival." But the Lord says, "No, neither is the great revival but both are steps towards it." When

45

the new church phase is on the wane, there will be evidenced in the churches something that has not been seen before: a coming together of those with an emphasis on the Word and those with an emphasis on the Spirit. When the Word and the Spirit come together, there will be the biggest movement of the Holy Spirit that the nation, and indeed the world, has ever seen. It will mark the beginning of a revival that will eclipse anything that has been witnessed within these shores, even the Wesleyan and the Welsh revivals of former years. The outpouring of God's Spirit will flow over from the UK to the mainland of Europe and from there will begin a missionary move to the ends of the earth.

reported prophecy of Smith Wigglesworth (1859–1947)
just before his death

There are three things I should say at the beginning of this chapter. First, this chapter is the substance of a talk I gave at the Wembley Conference Centre in London on October 16, 1992—titled at that time, "The Post-Charismatic Era." This message turned out to be the most controversial word I have given in 55 years of ministry.

Second, I had not heard of Smith Wigglesworth's 1947 prophecy until a day or two after my own talk at Wembley.

Third, I take "charismatic" to be shorthand for "Pentecostal," "apostolic," "neo-Pentecostal" (although I recognize some intricate and technical differences in these labels). All of these describe a contemporary movement that crosses denominational and theological lines and has been known for its emphasis on the gifts of the Holy Spirit—signs, wonders and miracles. It was known as the "glossalalia" movement in the 1960s (taken from the Greek glossa—"tongue" or "language") when the emphasis focused largely on speaking in tongues. It eventually became known as the charismatic movement—although the common denominator of this movement, according to recent polls, is now seen as the "prosperity gospel," not manifestations of the Spirit.

46

## Ishmael or Isaac?

A week before I gave the address at Wembley, I asked a leading British charismatic leader this question: "If the charismatic movement is either *Ishmael* or *Isaac,* which of these do you think it is?" He answered, "Isaac."

I replied: "If I told you that the charismatic movement is not Isaac but Ishmael, what would you think?" He answered, "I hope not."

I then said to him, "Your answer convinces me more than ever that the charismatic movement is Ishmael." Why so? His response was virtually the same as that of Abraham when informed that Ishmael was *not* the promised child but that Isaac was coming. Abraham wanted the promised child to be Ishmael—who was already around, alive and well. But no, Ishmael was not it. Isaac was coming, and the seed of Abraham (culminating in Jesus Christ) would go through Isaac.

What Abraham had wanted more than anything in the world—a son who came from Sarah's womb—was now being handed to him on a silver platter. But Abraham didn't want it! This is why he pleaded, "If only Ishmael might live under your blessing!" (Genesis 17:18). God was promising Abraham that a son would be born through his beloved Sarah. But things had changed. Abraham was rejecting God's promise in his heart!

Abraham would never have believed that he would react so negatively to something so positive: "As for Sarai your wife, you are no longer to call her Sarai; her name will be Sarah. I will bless her and will surely give you a son by her. I will bless her so that she will be the mother of nations; kings of peoples will come from her" (Genesis 17:15–16). But Abraham wanted Ishmael to be the promised child.

One could understand Abraham's feelings. They stemmed from the fact he had become attached to his beloved Ishmael and had by this time come to terms that Sarah would not conceive. Abraham's plea that Ishmael would be the promised son may also have arisen partly to vindicate his having slept with

Hagar thirteen years before: "If only Ishmael might live under your blessing!"

In much the same way, many people who are right in the middle of the charismatic movement want *it* to be the ultimate hope for the Church. They have paid a price for being a part of it, and it has not been easy. Some early Pentecostals saw themselves as the "latter rain," a movement said to come just before the Second Coming. Whatever name you wish to give it—latter rain or "last days ministries"—many charismatic Christians who are eschatologically minded have seen the charismatic movement as the ultimate and final hope for the Church prior to the Second Coming of Jesus. They therefore understandably want the movement of which they are a part to be that very phenomenon.

As a consequence of this type of thinking, many leaders of the British charismatic movement were livid with my word at Wembley on "The Post-Charismatic Era." One major charismatic leader wanted to call a national conference to sit in judgment on my prophetic word. Some of my very good friends left that meeting angry. The irony is that many evangelicals were also unhappy about my word—partly because I said that the Word and Spirit would come together in the coming of Isaac, but also because I had nice things to say about the charismatic movement!

### Abraham's Assumption about Ishmael

For thirteen years, Abraham sincerely believed that Ishmael was the promised son. It all began when God told Abraham that his seed would be as numerous as the stars in the heavens. Abraham had expressed concern that he had no heir and wondered if his servant Eliezer of Damascus would be the heir to his vast fortune. (Abraham was a very rich man.)

It was at this point God told Abraham, "This man will not be your heir, but a son who is your own flesh and blood will be your heir. . . . Count the stars—if indeed you can count them. . . . So shall your offspring be" (Genesis 15:4–5). The important thing is,

Abraham believed that word. He might have rejected it, saying, "Don't insult me with a preposterous word like that." But no, he believed it—*and Abraham's faith counted for righteousness* (Genesis 15:6). This meant that God would see Abraham as righteous from that day forward. This, as we saw above, became Paul's chief illustration for his doctrine of justification by faith alone (Romans 4). It is our Gospel to this very day!

Although Abraham really believed that promise, the years were rolling by and Sarah gave him no child. Abraham was getting older, Sarah was getting older, and no son was on the way. She had long before arrived at the age in which it is not possible for a woman to bear a child. Abraham and Sarah were discouraged. We all get discouraged when God does not seem to be keeping His word to us. We tend to fret during the time of unanswered prayer.

One day Sarah—not Abraham—came up with a solution. Sarah said to Abraham, "The LORD has kept me from having children. Go, sleep with my slave; perhaps I can build a family through her" (Genesis 16:2). Her maidservant was an Egyptian named Hagar. This was entirely Sarah's notion, and it was not a good idea.

Abraham, however, agreed to the proposition. After all, he really *did* believe the promise that God would give him an heir. He became willing to see it happen any way God chose to bring it about. What is more, if Hagar's child would be *male* it would indicate that God was truly at work. A male child would fit the description of Genesis 15:4—"a son who is your own flesh and blood will be your heir." God had said nothing about this child coming from Sarah's womb; Abraham merely assumed it would happen that way. But after a number of years of waiting—plus Sarah's suggestion—Abraham abandoned any hope of a son coming from Sarah's womb.

Abraham slept with Hagar, and she conceived. During the pregnancy, Sarah had second thoughts and began to despise Hagar. She also blamed Abraham for all that was going on. Abraham tried to be a peacemaker and said to Sarah, "Do with her whatever you think best." Sarah mistreated Hagar and Hagar fled.

An angel showed up near a spring in the desert where Hagar sat, telling her, "Go back to your mistress and submit to her. . . . I will increase your descendants so much that they will be too numerous to count. . . . You are now pregnant and you will give birth to a son. You shall name him Ishmael [meaning *God hears*], for the LORD has heard of your misery. He will be a wild donkey of a man; his hand will be against everyone and everyone's hand against him, and he will live in hostility toward all his brothers" (Genesis 16:9–12).

Hagar bore Abraham a son, and he gave the name Ishmael to Hagar's child. Abraham was 86 years old when Ishmael was born. Despite Sarah's efforts to hasten the promise of God, the seal of God was clearly on Ishmael's birth. Abraham could never forget this. As far as Abraham was concerned, God kept His word. It was perfectly clear to Abraham: *Ishmael* was the promised son that God had in mind all along.

### Abraham's Fervent Plea for Ishmael

One can easily appreciate Abraham's wish, "O that Ishmael might live before thee!" (Genesis 17:18, KJV). Abraham was not only reconciled to the suggestion that Hagar should be the mother of his son—it also met every condition of the promise of Genesis 15:4–6. All Abraham needed was to be sure the child of Hagar fit God's promise in this passage—and he did. As far as Abraham was concerned, the fulfillment of Genesis 15:4–6 was ancient history! It was *done*, over, end of story. God kept His word, and that was that. Ishmael met all the requirements, and Abraham had no complaints.

But God messed things up after Ishmael was 13 years old. One day, when Abraham was 99, he got up as he did any other morning. He was not prepared for what would happen on that day. Out of the blue God appeared to Abraham and said: "I am God Almighty; walk before me faithfully and be blameless. Then

I will make my covenant between me and you and will greatly increase your numbers" (Genesis 17:1–2).

Abraham fell facedown. Whereas he had been called Abram up to now, he was given the name Abraham, "for I have made you a father of many nations. . . . The whole land of Canaan, where you now reside as a foreigner, I will give as an everlasting possession to you and your descendants after you; and I will be their God" (Genesis 17:5, 8).

Then came instructions about circumcision. Every male among Abraham's extended family would be circumcised. Not only that, but "you are to undergo circumcision" (Genesis 17:11).

### Surprising News

But there was more. Sarai was to be given the name Sarah. Not only that, "I will bless her and will surely *give you a son by her.* I will bless her so that she will be the mother of nations; kings of peoples will come from her" (Genesis 17:15–16, emphasis mine).

Abraham's first reaction was to fall facedown and *laugh*. He said to himself, "Will a son be born to a man a hundred years old? Will Sarah bear a child at the age of ninety?" But the implications set in and he offered a fervent plea: "If only Ishmael might live under your blessing!" (Genesis 17:18).

Abraham may have been perfectly fine about Sarah having a child, but his deepest fear at this juncture was that it would be Sarah's child—not Hagar's—through whom the covenant promise would come. His fears were founded. God gave Abraham instructions: "You will call him Isaac [meaning *he laughs*]. I will establish my covenant with him as an everlasting covenant for his descendants after him. And as for Ishmael, I have heard you: I will surely bless him. . . . *But my covenant I will establish with Isaac,* whom Sarah will bear to you by this time next year" (Genesis 17:19–21, emphasis mine).

Abraham accepted the new word from God. He also circumcised Ishmael. Abraham not only believed what God said to him

51

regarding Isaac, "Yet he did not waver through unbelief regarding the promise of God, but was strengthened in his faith and gave glory to God, being fully persuaded that God had power to do what he had promised" (Romans 4:20–21).

## Is God Saying This Again—To Us?

What I stated at the Wembley Conference Centre on the night of October 16, 1992, I now repeat: *This is precisely what I believe God is saying to us today.* Sarah will conceive. Isaac is coming. However much we love Ishmael, however much people may love the Pentecostal-charismatic movement, however much God affirmed Ishmael, however much Ishmael fits the promise—God is up to something *new.* Although God is behind Ishmael, Ishmael is not the ultimate fulfillment of the promise. Sarah will conceive—Isaac is on the way.

Does this make you sad? Why was Abraham sad? He should not have been, although he was at first. Perhaps you, too—if charismatic—have hoped that what has been going on over the past generation was "it." If so, you may be a little sad that this is not "it."

And yet if Ishmael could give Abraham so much joy, how much more did Isaac? If Ishmael has been blessed of God, how much more is Isaac? When we consider how God has blessed the Church through the charismatic movement and how many wonderful and thrilling things have come during the Pentecostal and charismatic era, *what will Isaac be like?*

## Why Affirm the Charismatic Era?

Why should the charismatic era be affirmed—and affirmed by evangelicals?

First, Abraham did not initiate the era of Ishmael. Abraham was an honorable man, believing God's promise. Sarah—"our mother" (Galatians 4:26)—was the instigator of the whole thing. And yet it came to Abraham as a word from God.

Make no mistake: The charismatic era is what God did. We the Church are generally all the better for the charismatic movement. As for Britain, where I served as a pastor for much of this era, most churches there worth their salt are largely charismatic. Alpha, one of the greatest evangelistic enterprises ever to come along, was born in Holy Trinity Brompton, one of London's best-known charismatic Anglican churches.

The greatest hymns of the past thirty years have been authored and composed by those people who are right in the middle of the charismatic movement. Try to find a "non-charismatic" (if I may use that phrase) hymn that has been written and widely sung in the past thirty years—it is rare. Not only that, the spreading of Christianity in the Third World—Africa (where Christianity is growing faster than Islam), Latin America, Indonesia, South America and Korea—is typified by what most would call either charismatic or Pentecostal. One evidence of this is that most Christians in the Third World speak in tongues.

A second reason why the charismatic movement should be appreciated and affirmed by evangelicals is because Sarah "our mother" persecuted Hagar. Have you any idea just how much charismatic Christians have suffered—not only in the world, but also by the hands of non-charismatic Christians? Pentecostals and neo-Pentecostals—those who dare talk about gifts of the Spirit, signs and wonders and miracles—have been "outside the camp" like Hagar in the desert (Hebrews 13:13). They have been ridiculed by non-charismatics and evangelicals, lied about, misunderstood and—in some places—persecuted as much as in any era of the Christian Church. In America, so it seems to me, the charismatic movement is seen as the lunatic fringe of the Church (although the movement is quite mainstream in Britain). I know churches where the sin of adultery would be more readily forgiven than if one spoke in tongues.

A third reason to affirm the charismatic movement: Hagar was affirmed by an undoubted divine visitation in the desert. She could look up to God through her tears and say, "You are the God who sees me" ["Thou God seest me"] (Genesis 16:13, KJV). She knew one thing: God gave her a son and *God named him*. Remember, Ishmael means "God hears." God left Hagar with no doubt that He was with her and behind it all. Likewise, those who unashamedly call themselves charismatics know that God has visited them, affirmed them and blessed them, and some of them have seen the supernatural. Don't tell me it is all spurious, that their claims are always unfounded or that all they do is get worked up. It is simply not so.

A fourth reason to affirm the movement: God had a secret purpose for Ishmael that was revealed first to Hagar and later to Abraham. The angel of the Lord said to Hagar, "I will so increase your descendants that they will be too numerous to count" (Genesis 16:10). God said the same thing later on to Abraham: "I will make him [Ishmael] fruitful and will greatly increase his numbers. . . . I will make him into a great nation" (Genesis 17:20). What is more, we have not seen the end of this. The natural literal Arabic descendants of Ishmael are too numerous to count. They have inhabited Britain and America in ever-increasing numbers. Their mosques and places of worship are going up in rapid fashion in every major city in Europe and America. Who knows what the end will be?

But I predict: We are going to see Islam turning to Jesus Christ in massive numbers before the end. Count on it. Muslims turning to Christ could even be the catalyst that will wake up Jews all over the world. After all, Paul hoped that the conversion of Gentiles would "arouse" Jews to envy "and save some of them" (Romans 11:14). In any case, the coming of Isaac will bring with it the lifting of the blindness that is on Israel to this day (Romans 11:8, 25). "What no eye has seen, what no ear has heard, and what no human mind has conceived—the things God has prepared for those who love him" (1 Corinthians 2:9).

## What the Promise of Isaac Did for Abraham

Why was Ishmael not meant to be the promised child? It is, first of all, because God wanted the promise of the Gospel as revealed to Abraham to be fulfilled in a manner that *defied a natural explanation*. When Hagar conceived it was not exactly a miracle. Ishmael's birth had a very natural explanation. But when Sarah conceived there was no doubt: Only God could have done this!

Second, God wanted the heirs of the Gospel to look back on what He did in a manner no one could question. Understandable though it was for Abraham to agree to Sarah's proposal that he sleep with Hagar, there would always be a cloud over it, a nagging doubt. Even Abraham must have questioned: Was sleeping with Hagar *really* what God had in mind? Is that all there is to the promise God gave to me that my seed would be as numerous as the stars in the heavens? Is that what God had in mind when I was counted righteous?

I don't mean to be unfair, but though the presence of the supernatural is not to be denied in some quarters of the charismatic movement, one must admit that real, undoubted and empirical proof of most claims to signs and wonders today are often unverifiable. This is what is so disappointing. Real miracles are not very common, especially in Britain and America. Of course, there are exceptions. But the very fact that, sadly, the charismatic movement's common denominator is no longer manifestations of the Spirit but the "prosperity" message is a dead giveaway that miracles are not happening much after all. There never would have been a shift away from signs and wonders to an emphasis on jobs and money had undoubted miracles been in abundance. This shift has to be one of the most melancholy turns of events ever.

A third reason why Ishmael was not meant to be the promised child: What is often overlooked is that the promise of Isaac drove Abraham back to God's word. The apostle Paul makes this point. Abraham had been credited with righteousness by his faith. But it was coming to terms with the original promise regarding his seed that made him eventually leap at the new promise regarding Sarah.

> Against all hope, Abraham in hope believed and so became the father of many nations, just as it had been said to him, "So shall your offspring be." Without weakening in his faith, he faced the fact that his body was as good as dead—since he was about a hundred years old—and that Sarah's womb was also dead. Yet he did not waver through unbelief regarding the promise of God, but was strengthened in his faith and gave glory to God, being fully persuaded that God had power to do what he had promised. This is why "it was credited to him as righteousness."
>
> Romans 4:18–22

Abraham had understood the word—the dignity and glory of it. But with the promise of Isaac on the way—once he became reconciled to it—Abraham was driven back to the word God had given him, a word that gave him full assurance.

I predict: If we will accept this word that I am putting to you in this chapter, many will get back to the Word of God as they have not done in years. There will be a new romance with Scriptures—like falling in love all over again. It will result in a fresh assurance, just like that of Abraham in Romans 4. We will have something to live for unlike what we have ever had.

A fourth reason why Ishmael would not fulfill the promise: The post-charismatic era will be characterized by an awe with regard to the Word that is equal to the awe we think we now have toward the supernatural. I'm sorry—I wish it were not so—but I fear that few of us truly experience a holy awe with reference to the Word—by which I mean the Bible.

When I hear so many modern songs, so shallow and devoid of sound theology, as I go from church to church (some of which are charismatic), I die a thousand deaths. It is said that the early Methodists got their theology from their hymns. And when you look at the hymns of Isaac Watts and Charles Wesley, you can see why God blessed the early Methodists. Then compare the classic hymns with what is being sung in many places nowadays, and you see why there is such shallowness and superficiality: There is virtually no theology.

When the Word and Spirit coalesce, this is the essence of the coming of Isaac. It is a remarriage of that which God has said the following will take place: "What therefore God hath joined together, let not man put asunder" (Matthew 19:6, KJV). By Word I do mean good theology; by Spirit I mean His manifest presence. Sound teaching combined with the manifest presence of the Holy Spirit will send a signal that Isaac has come. It will not get better than that.

**What Is Good Theology?**

On the morning following my original talk at the Wembley Conference Centre in 1992, I received a phone call from a prominent charismatic leader in London. He rather urgently wanted to know if by "Word and Spirit coming together" I meant Reformed theology with the manifest presence of the Spirit?

He himself was not Reformed and knew that I was. He was accepting what I stated about the coming of Isaac, but he was also very concerned lest I was predicting that the Word would be a vindication of Reformed theology. His call gave me pause and I have thought a lot about this. In other words, when the Word and Spirit coalesce with unprecedented power, will this mean that classical Calvinism takes over? No. In a word: I would not push the finer points of Reformed theology too far. I have watched churches die overnight where this has been done.

I am only sure of one thing: The book of Romans, with special reference to Romans 4 (which is about justification by faith and our coming into our inheritance), will be the theological common denominator in the "Isaac" era. I doubt it will cross many minds whether it is "Reformed." But I can guarantee that the Gospel of Jesus Christ will be back on the map.

The Gospel turned the world upside down in the sixteenth century. John Wesley's discovery of Martin Luther's views on justification turned his own life upside down—and England was not to be the same again after that for a good while. Sadly, that Gospel has passed behind a cloud in Europe and America. The true Gospel has been largely eclipsed by sterile orthodoxy in some quarters, a denial of the reliability of Scripture in others and an emphasis on prosperity where Christian television has held sway. This will change.

Two things will be at the forefront when it comes to teaching and preaching in the era of "Isaac": (1) a restoration of the Gospel—doctrine of justification by faith alone—and (2) a widespread appreciation and acceptance of (and adherence to) the sovereignty of God.

## Justification by Faith

We begin with what happened when Jesus died on the cross. Two things essentially took place on Good Friday: *expiation*—what the blood of Jesus does for us, namely, it washes away our sins—and *propitiation*—what the blood of Jesus does for God.

We are living at a time when most preaching caters to people's "what's in it for me?" mentality. When it comes to the cross of Jesus Christ, most people do not get past the issue of what the blood does for *us*—the atonement for our sins. But there would be no atonement if *God Himself* had not been appeased by Jesus' death. Propitiation means that the blood of Jesus turned the Father's wrath away from our sins and that God was satisfied, or appeased, by Jesus' death on the cross.

Sadly, most people do not give much thought to what Jesus' atonement did for God. But they should. Indeed, they should be most grateful for this aspect of the cross: God the Father being *satisfied* by the perfect life and sacrificial death of His Son, Jesus Christ. This is *the reason* we can be sure our sins have been washed away.

58

The promise is this: All who transfer their hope in their own good works to what Jesus did for them on the cross will be saved. The moment they rely totally and solely on Jesus' blood, God credits them with *righteousness*. Just as Abraham believed the promise and it meant that the righteousness was imputed to him, so it is when people today believe the Gospel, righteousness is imputed to them (Romans 4:5). It is their *faith alone* that did it—not their works. God Almighty declares such people just or righteous—owing to their sheer faith in Jesus' blood. Their works do not come into the picture at all.

I have made an astonishing discovery in the past few years. Perhaps it should not have surprised me, but it did. I often ask congregations: "If you stood before God (and you will) and He were to ask you (and He might), 'Why should I let you into My heaven?' what would you say?" I have them write their answer down on a sheet of paper, then I read their answers later. It is sobering to discover how many of them have been trusting in their own efforts and not solely in the death of Jesus. In fact, the numbers are staggering. Sometimes over 50 percent of a congregation reveal their trust is in something other than the death of Jesus Christ. This discloses a very sad fact: The Gospel had not been grasped by them!

This, too, will change. When "Isaac" comes, the Gospel will be central. The cross will become the focus. The person of Jesus will become the object of their enthrallment. People will run to teaching and preaching in order to hear the Word of God made simple and clear. The Bible's infallibility will be an assumption. People will hang on to every word. The hunger for the Word will transcend their "what's in it for me?" preoccupation.

## The Sovereignty of God

But there is more. The feeling of "entitlement" that has governed the hearts of many people in our generation will be replaced by an awareness that God owes us nothing. Instead of people being told they can demand that God give them what they want—and that God is obligated to give them what they want—men and women will come to Him on bended knee, knowing they cannot snap their fingers before a sovereign God and expect Him to jump. The same God who said to Moses, "I will have mercy on whom I will have mercy" (Exodus 33:19; Romans 9:15), is the same God we pray to—the Father of our Lord Jesus Christ.

The leper came to Jesus not snapping his finger, demanding that he be saluted, but only said, "Lord, if *you are willing* [because you don't have to], you can make me clean" (Matthew 8:2, emphasis mine). The leper knew his place in that society. We will know our place, too. "For just as the Father raises the dead and gives them life, even so the Son gives life to whom he is pleased to give it" (John 5:21). "No one knows the Son except the Father, and no one knows the Father except the Son and those to whom the Son chooses to reveal him" (Matthew 11:27).

We will be conscious that God is sovereign and that we are beggars. A touch of that consciousness was present when Jonathan Edwards preached his sermon "Sinners in the Hands of an Angry God" in Enfield, Connecticut, in 1741. Strong men were seen holding on to tree trunks to keep from falling into hell. The coming of "Isaac" will be a restoration of an awareness of God's sovereignty.

The truth is, we cannot make God do anything. We cannot make Him save people. We cannot make Him heal people. We must be like the leper: "Lord, *if You will*, You can heal me." But when people fancy they can have so much faith that they can heal anybody they wish, they betray their ignorance of the ways of the God of the Bible.

Not all have faith. Only God can give faith. He can give it or withhold it and be just either way. As John the Baptist put it, "A person can receive only what is given them from heaven" (John 3:27). That is what I mean by the sovereignty of God. It will make us lower our voices. It will put God on His throne, us on our knees.

## Signs, Wonders and Miracles

But there is still more. This immaculate Word will be joined by the omnipotent Holy Spirit. Miracles will take place before people's eyes. There will not only be the conversion of the most unlikely people, there will be healing of the most helpless people.

God will show His power in a way so obvious that it will be said again, "Everyone . . . knows they have done an outstanding miracle, and we cannot deny it" (Acts 4:16). It should not be surprising if God raised the dead, just to show His ability before a doubting and lost generation. Yes, it *will* be reported in *The New York Times*. They will have no choice but to report this sort of thing. Miracles in the "Isaac" era will not be done in a corner; the whole world will be affected by it.

God will raise up leaders who will stand where no one has stood since the days of the early Church. We will be back in the book of Acts—possibly witnessing things that exceed what is described there. Yes, Isaac is coming!

## What Will the "Coming of Isaac" Be Like?

The promise concerning Isaac was far greater than the promise about Ishmael. The consequences of the coming of "Isaac," then, will be in proportion to the greater glory given to Isaac compared to the promise pertaining to Ishmael. In a word: The power and glory in the coming movement will be incalculably greater than anything seen in the past century.

It will be an era in which the Word preached will be even more awesome than the vindication of God's name that is manifest through miracles. However startling these healings and miracles—and they will be manifest—it will be the Word that will dazzle people most. I am describing an era in which signs and wonders will not be under a cloud of suspicion but will be open to the minutest scrutiny by the harshest critic. The conclusion will be: "We cannot deny it."

And yet it will be a time when the Gospel—not prosperity teaching or bizarre interpretations of the Bible—is the front-runner of priorities among God's ministers. It will be a time when conversions to Christ will not be minimized but seen as the greatest miracle that can happen under the sun. And yet it will be a time when the most difficult cases imaginable will be turned into putty in the hands of a sovereign God. Scientists, philosophers, psychologists, atheists, infidels, bankers and politicians who scoffed will be mollified, humbled and made to bow at the feet of the sovereign Redeemer. Surprising conversions will be common. But not everybody will be saved.

It will be an era when worldly people will fear the prayers of God's people more than they fear nuclear war. It is said that Mary Queen of Scots feared the prayers of John Knox more than the king's armies. It will be an era when government and people in highest places will come on bended knee to God's people to ask for help.

With Ishmael it was a promise of a nation; with Isaac, the promise of many nations. Yes, Abraham's seed would be "heir of the world" (Romans 4:13). Indeed, we are talking about something *big*—huge. It is something far wider than America's boundaries, far beyond Britain's shores. Kings of the earth, leaders of nations and the rich and famous of this world will be made to see there is a God in the heavens.

It will be an era in which children will be sovereign vessels. It will be an era in which ordinary Christians will be equipped with prophetic and miraculous gifts. Instead of religious superstars vying for TV time—trying to be seen or heard or to prove themselves—it will be unknown servants of God taking the lead out in the open.

In a word: It will be that era foreseen by the prophets when the knowledge of the glory of the Lord will cover the earth as the waters cover the sea (Isaiah 11:9; Habakkuk 2:14). What was foretold by the prophets will come true—and this day will come *before* the Second Coming of Jesus.

How far away is this? Not far. How long will it be? Not long. Habakkuk said that the revelation "awaits an appointed time; it speaks of the end and will not prove false. Though it linger, wait for it; it will certainly come and will not delay" (Habakkuk 2:3). Abraham pleaded, "If only Ishmael might live under your blessing!" (Genesis 17:18).

If only. But no, Isaac is coming! Isaac means "he laughs." The laughter heard at that time will not be the laughter of cynicism, as Abraham laughed initially at God's promise. All scoffing then will turn to reverent fear—when the honor of God's name at long last will be restored.

# PART TWO

# SPIRIT

## JACK TAYLOR

four

# My Testimony:
# Who Is This Stranger?

He has been the object of many discussions, the alleged reason for many divisions and the most feared person of the Trinity. At the same time He is the most ignored and taken for granted. Those reckless enough and bold enough to speak or write about Him should be prepared for criticism from many who disagree on any detail. He has been called the Forgotten God, the most important Person on earth, the only God on the planet, the Phantom God, the here-and-now God, God where it counts, the Paraclete (one called alongside), Heaven's Throne Gift and a plethora of other names.

Though He was sent to unify the Church and to provide it with enablement to accomplish its intended purpose, He has been at the center of as much division and controversy as any other subject in Church history. The very mention of His name— "Holy Spirit"—stirs contention in many quarters.

Who is this Stranger, anyway? How can we walk through the minefield of Holy Spirit information without offending many?

I sincerely doubt if such a project is possible. The Holy Spirit is the Third Person of the Trinity, coequal and cooperative with God the Father and God the Son. In God's order of things in history, the Father sent the Son, and when the Son had died and was resurrected He returned to the Father. It was then that the Father and Son sent the Holy Spirit.

When I was a boy, we had only the King James Version of the Bible, in which the Holy Spirit is referred to as the Holy Ghost. Not being into ghosts all that seriously, and possessing both misinformation on one hand and next to none on the other, I had an aversion to this Stranger—a decisive prejudice, if you please.

I accepted Jesus Christ as my Savior when I was ten years of age. The subject of the Holy Spirit (or Holy Ghost) was not mentioned as being important enough to consider in my Baptist upbringing. The Pentecostal group on the hill in my little town was the object of much humor and was thought to be so weird that conventional wisdom was to leave them alone. Yet this was not humorous to me—it was fearful!

The fact that I had no background teaching on the Holy Spirit put me at a disadvantage to approach the subject with any degree of openness to Him. Added to this disadvantage was a fear that developed in me that prejudiced me against Him. Another problem, which I will not detail here, caused my fear to be even more pronounced. I promise you: It was no little fear, it was near terror.

I knew I was born again, saved and would go to heaven when I died, though there were brief times of recurring doubt. Had I been asked at the time if I thought this was all there was to Christianity, I would have had to answer, "Goodness, I hope not!"

## Called to Preach

Four years after I was saved, I felt a strange moving in my teenage heart. When my pastor made a special visit to our country home, acting on what I would have called at the time a spiritual "hunch," he asked me if I had felt the call to preach. Almost before I thought, my answer was, "Yes!" He had hit the nail right on the head. I have never once doubted my call to preach. While that fact may not seem strange to you, let me add that I had doubted my salvation.

Looking back later, I asked myself, "Why was there doubt about my salvation?" This is what I discovered: When I made the decision to "accept Christ as Savior," that's all there was to it. In fact, I'm not even sure that is what our church called what I was doing.

Most of the people saved in my hometown Baptist church were saved during the "summer revival," a phrase only half of which was accurate. It did take place in the summer but was not a revival by any stretch of the imagination. "Revival" was just a title we gave to an annual series of meetings every year. A couple of my friends and I decided to make our decisions together in the Tuesday morning service of the so-called revival. We stood near the front to make it easy if not inevitable. When the invitation was given, however, my friends stepped back immediately and I was left standing alone. This was more serious to me than simply deciding to join the church. In a moment, I stepped out into the aisle and was greeted by the pastor.

In my ten-year-old mind I was saying "yes" to Jesus and that was that. No one thought to tell me what had happened to me. I don't even remember anyone praying with me. I was given no memory pegs on which to hang my experience, no explanation of these new feelings I was having and no idea of what to do with the Jesus I had opened my young heart to receive. I believed both then and now that all it takes to be saved is to call on Jesus—but while that is true, there must be more for a life of peace, success and victory. I know now that this "more" we are discussing involves a full-blown pursuit of the ministry of the Third Person of the Trinity, the Holy Spirit.

My tender heart was fertile soil for the sowing of doubt that plagued me for years. Then one day I simply said to God,

"Father, I cannot remember what I prayed that morning, or whether it was even adequate. But if it did not happen on that Tuesday morning, I am asking You to seal it now and certify my salvation. I am driving a stake here, right now, to remind me that my salvation is settled."

I now know that what happened that day was initiated by none other than the Holy Spirit, who worked in me despite my quiet fear of Him. I did not even have a Scripture for this assuring experience but later stumbled across 1 John 4:13: "This is how we know that we live in him and he in us: He has given us of his Spirit."

When I was called to preach, I was a fourteen-year-old country boy. I was so green that if I had stood still I would have sprouted (one of many country sayings familiar in those now ancient days). So here I was, saved and now called to preach, and I remember distinctly two encounters I had within days of my responding to the call.

The first was my atheist uncle trying to shake my young faith in the existence of God by asking what came before the beginning. With no training in debate and certainly no knowledge of theology, I remember saying, "If God had been interested in our knowing the answer to that question, He would have said in Genesis 1:1, 'Before the beginning . . .'" I tell this now realizing it was not an arrogant answer but one the Holy Spirit gave me without my being aware!

The second experience was a minor confrontation with my grandma, who as I remember, rest her soul, was not the kindest person in the neighborhood. She peered at me through her coke-bottle spectacles and, speaking in harsh tones, said, "You gonna preach?" I answered in the affirmative. She continued, "You got the Holy Ghost?" I answered more slowly, "Well, I think I do." She furthered her inquisition, "Did you speak in tongues?" Now, my affirmatives ceased: "Not that I know of." That was my first experience of the idea that the Holy Spirit and tongues went together. But I vowed silently to myself that I would seek out this issue until I could answer it more correctly.

Grandma died before I could properly answer that question. I feel I should go further down this road to tell you that Grandpa was one of the godliest people I ever knew, but according to Grandma he did not have the Holy Spirit because he had never spoken in tongues. I knew him as a sweet, kind and all-around nice guy, while Grandma was rather cantankerous, to put it mildly. I will never forget Grandpa's funeral, where his body lay for viewing with an open Bible lying on his still chest. I highly favored Grandpa over Grandma. So put another mark on the negative side to my Holy Spirit experience in those years.

These details may not seem particularly relevant for our subject. But I mention them because in my experience many have had similar Holy Spirit hang-ups—and that may include many reading this book.

### An Inquiring Mind Needing to Know

I preached my first sermon over six decades ago at the age of fourteen. I desired to be the best preacher I could be, so despite my fears of the Trinity's Third Person, I began to read biographies of the most famous preachers of the past. In most of these biographies one thing stood out: an encounter with the Holy Spirit after the salvation experience. It happened to Jonathan Edwards, John and Charles Wesley, Charles Grandison Finney, F. B. Meyer, A. B. Simpson, A. W. Tozer, Charles Haddon Spurgeon and many others.

I began to ask, investigate and study the Scriptures only to discover that such an experience was indeed scriptural. Paul was saved on the Damascus road and filled with the Spirit on Straight Street in Damascus under the influence (and laying on of hands) of Ananias. The disciples received the Spirit when Jesus breathed on them and said, "Receive the Holy Spirit" (John 20:22). Later, in Acts 2, on the Day of Pentecost, everyone in the crowd of 120—doubtlessly including the remaining disciples—were baptized and filled with the Spirit.

These and many other stories of men and women in Church history encountering the Holy Spirit helped me begin to move past my fears into a measure of openness. One obvious problem: I was Baptist, and Baptists did not speak of the Holy Spirit much at all. They especially avoided any attention to the gifts of the Spirit. (Remember, we are talking about conditions more than half a century ago.)

During my early seminary career I noticed that there were no required courses on the Holy Spirit. I examined the curriculum catalog, found a course entitled "The Person and Work of the Holy Spirit" and excitedly signed up for it. The author of the course textbook was an eminent and widely respected Baptist theologian, and the teacher of the class was one of the most popular professors in the seminary—so I felt very safe as I began the class.

As I remember, the class proceeded as a wonderful experience and I looked forward to going. My imagination naively soared to expect the day when our teacher would tell us how to be filled with the Spirit, how to be led by the Spirit, how to continue being filled with the Spirit and how to walk and minister in the Spirit's power, wisdom and anointing. I anticipated our much-loved and deeply studious professor coming to class one day with a noticeably sly grin coupled with an air of anticipation. He would say:

"Now, my young friends, today we are going to discuss our personal relationship with this wonderful Person, the Spirit of God. The apostle Paul, our greatest theologian, said in Ephesians 5:15–18, 'Be very careful, then, how you live—not as unwise but as wise, making the most of every opportunity, because the days are evil. Therefore do not be foolish, but understand what the Lord's will is. Do not get drunk on wine, which leads to debauchery. Instead, be filled with the Spirit.'"

I am sorry to say, the promised discussion never happened—the one about our personal relationship with this wonderful Person. Though hugely impressed with good information about the Holy Spirit, I found the class to be much like my experience with the frog in freshman biology lab in college. We were given a dead frog, marinated in formaldehyde, as our lab companion for the course. We would study its skin and appendages and record comments on the frog's external features. Then, in a later lab, we would skin the frog and begin a study of the muscles, brain, lungs and (ugh) stomach. Finally, we would strip all the flesh from the bones, leave the skeleton to dry and tie it to a cardboard square.

When all was said and done, we knew much about the frog—but we did not know the frog at all. At the end of the course on the Holy Spirit, I knew much about the Holy Spirit—but, sadly, I did not know the Holy Spirit personally.

### Resumé of the Holy Spirit

In those days, many folks had the bad habit of speaking of the Holy Spirit as an "it"—which He most certainly is not. He is a person with a personality, with the feelings and characteristics of a person. He—a person like Jesus and like the Father—represents both on earth so uniquely that they can be spoken of as being here in the Holy Spirit. Consider the following passage in John 14:15–21:

> If you love me, keep my commands. And I will ask the Father, and he will give you another advocate to help you and be with you forever—The Spirit of truth. The world cannot accept him, because it neither sees him nor knows him. But you know him, for he lives with you and will be in you. I will not leave you as orphans; I will come to you. Before long, the world will not see me anymore, but you will see me. Because I live, you also will live. On that day you will realize that I am in my Father, and you are in me, and I am in you. Whoever has my commands and keeps them is the one who loves me. He who loves me will be loved by my Father, and I too will love them and show myself to them.

73

It is very clear through this passage that the work of Father and Son continues on earth after the coming of the Holy Spirit. They are there in heaven at the throne but also here—there but here! They are no less there because they are here, and no less here because they are there. There and here!

Blessed mystery, blessed Holy Spirit. It is by the Spirit that Jesus is in the Father. And we are in Jesus and He is in us by the same means: the Holy Spirit! Jesus, as He walked on earth, could never have lived in us, even in His resurrected body. God the Father remains on the throne in heaven, with the resurrected Jesus at His right hand. Only the Holy Spirit is here, and He is in us, the redeemed.

In summary, this Stranger is none other than the Holy Spirit, the Third Person of the Trinity. He is a person and He is here; He is God here and He is Jesus here. He is Comforter and counselor, one called alongside.

In John 14 and 16 Jesus gives the history of the Holy Spirit prophetically. He is careful to leave nothing in doubt about the coming of the Spirit after He, Jesus, ascends to heaven. I would urge you to stop here and read John 14:15–31, 15:26–27 and 16:5–16. You will notice some obvious points of light on this One who has become a Stranger to many. Consider some of these:

He is called "Counselor" in the Greek language in which the New Testament was originally written. The word used here is *Paraclete*, a combination of two words literally translated "one called alongside" (John 14:15–16).

His coming was to be a joint endeavor of both Father and Son: "I will ask the Father, and he will give you another advocate to be with you forever" (John 14:16).

He is called also the Spirit of truth—thus we may consider that among His main purposes will be "traffic director" on the journey of truth (John 14:17).

Jesus makes clear that, though He is leaving them, the disciples will not be left orphans: "I will come to you"—a veiled promise that in the coming of the Holy Spirit, He, Jesus, will still be with them, though unseen. "Before long the world will not see me anymore, but you will see me. Because I live, you also will live." One of the greatest points of light of this passage is in John 14:20: "On that day you will realize that I am in my Father, and you are in me, and I am in you."

The "day" referred to here marks the coming of the Spirit at Pentecost. Though it is not specifically recorded in the story of Pentecost in Acts 2, we may be sure that every person in that Upper Room, caught in the tornado-like wind of the Spirit's coming and filled with the Spirit, knew by spiritual instinct that whatever was happening here involved the total Trinity—God the Father, Jesus Christ the Son and the Holy Spirit. This is clear in a later verse, John 14:23: "Anyone who loves me will obey my teaching. My Father will love them, and we will come to them and make our home with them."

Thus, we safely conclude that Jesus was making clear that the coming of the Spirit would involve the coming of the Father and Son. This fact must never be forgotten or taken for granted. In this age of the Spirit, He will represent fully the presence of Father and Son.

## A Silent Theft

At some unknown, undetected juncture in Church history there seemed to be a loss of awareness of the presence of this wondrous Heavenly Guest. Though present, His place in Christianity has at times been seen as vague, surrounded by doubt and even fear. Across the years the Spirit has been recognized, though without clear information as to His purpose and place in the Church.

Despite this, every major statement of Christian faith includes a confession of faith in the person of the Holy Spirit. While not much information is given beyond a statement that equates His importance with God the Father and God the Son, Jesus Christ, He is at least mentioned in these confessions. His treatment in the following two are typical.

## 1. *The New Hampshire Baptist Confession*

In the New Hampshire Baptist Confession, 1833—one of the better known confessions—we read under the subject "Of the True God" (all emphasis mine):

We believe that there is one, and only one, living and true God,

An infinite, *intelligent Spirit,* whose name is Jehovah, the Maker and Supreme Ruler of Heaven and earth, inexpressibly glorious

In holiness, and worthy of all possible honor, confidence and love,

That in the unity of the Godhead there are three persons, the Father, the Son, and the *Holy Ghost,* equal in every divine perfection and executing distinct and harmonious offices in the great work of redemption.

Then again, under the subject "Of Grace in Regeneration" we read:

We believe that, in order to be saved, sinners must be regenerated, or born again; that regeneration consists in giving a holy disposition of the mind; that it is

Affected in a manner above our comprehension by

The power of the *Holy Spirit,* in connection with divine truth.

We read under the division "Of Sanctification":

We believe that Sanctification is the process by which, according to the will of God, we are made partakers of his holiness; that it is a progressive work;

That it is begun in regeneration; and that it is carried on in the hearts of believers by the presence and power of *the Holy Spirit, the Sealer and Comforter,* in the continual use of appointed means—especially the Word of God, self-examination, self-denial, watchfulness and prayer.

76

Once more, under the subject "Of the Righteous and the Wicked," we read:

We believe that there is a radical difference between the righteous and the wicked; that such only as are justified in the name of the Lord Jesus, and sanctified by the *Spirit of God,* are truly righteous in his esteem.

These several mentions of the Holy Ghost (i.e., Holy Spirit) form the extent of the information on the subject found in the well-known New Hampshire Baptist Confession of Faith, 1833.

## 2. The Westminster Confession

Worthy of mention is the brief statement in The Westminster Confession under the subject "Of God and of the Holy Trinity":

In the unity of the Godhead there are three Persons of one substance, power and eternity; God the Father, God the Son and God the Holy Ghost. The Father is of none, neither begotten nor proceeding; the Son is eternally begotten of the Father; the Holy Ghost eternally proceeding from the Father and the Son.

The general scarcity of specific information on the Holy Spirit in our traditional confessions of faith through the years stirs little controversy. What is there is basic and foundational. However, to give ourselves an advantage regarding the Person, work and ministry of this Third Person of the Trinity, we must dare to enter the subjects with boldness and openness. We must fully expect and be prepared for differing opinions, set traditions and continuing conflict. Be assured that though entry into such a study is sometimes painful, it will walk us down a path leading to great reward.

It is our studied opinion and conviction as coauthors in the "Word, Spirit, Power" team—R. T. Kendall, Charles Carrin and myself, Jack Taylor—that when we recover the original purpose of the Holy Spirit's coming to earth, we will also have recovered the path to true spiritual renewal. This renewal comes in experiencing the power of God and astounding success in bringing people to faith in Jesus. In the process, we will be driven to our knees, giving glad consent that the God who created this universe, the Christ who died for us and was raised from the dead and the Spirit who fueled the first-century Church and gave the gospel of the Kingdom to the world, form the only hope for our divided, devastated and distressed world.

## The Proper Order

In the days prior to our launching the ministry of "Word Spirit Power" conferences, we felt that this order of the three—the Word, the Holy Spirit and Power—was the only correct and workable sequence. What we know of the Spirit comes from the Word, our base and source of all valid information. The Word must be kept foremost, and there should be no room for "private interpretation." While the Word is clearly elevated even above the name of God (Psalm 138:2, KJV), its continuing credibility and life-giving power are dependent on the Holy Spirit. Neither is sufficient for life and ministry without the other. If we have the Word without the Spirit, we tend to "dry up"; if we have the Spirit without the Word, we tend to "blow up"; if we have both Spirit and Word, we tend to "grow up" and "fire up." But when each is properly joined in common union, there is explosive power to be had.

five

# Filled with the Spirit

In every generation there arises a hunger for more in the spiritual life. The more pressing the external conditions and internal emotions, the more extensive is this hunger for more of God. When conditions are formed by multiple crises—locally, regionally, nationally and internationally—the hunger component seems to rise.

The 21st century arrived with thunderous threats from every direction, and it is commonly agreed that we face an unprecedented global crisis. Personal and corporate anxiety is on the rise, with desperation flanking us on every side. Economic collapse threatens not only individuals but whole regions as well as the entire global family. Frustration and anger are common among the nations.

In the United States especially, local communities find themselves under a cloud of oppression. Meanwhile, churches are failing to address the cultural and social issues that threaten their very existence. Bent more on survival than success, we seem to lack both heart and power to recover the glory of the church of Acts.

What a time to return to God and the Bible! Such times have occurred throughout history, biblical and secular. Times of drought, plague, war and calamity have prompted times of spiritual awakening. The historical disposition of God is registered in 2 Chronicles 7:12–14:

> I have heard your prayer and have chosen this place for myself as a temple of sacrifices. When I shut up the heavens so that there is no rain, or command locusts to devour the land or send a plague among my people, if my people, who are called by my name, will humble themselves and pray and seek my face and turn from their wicked ways, then will I hear from heaven, and will forgive their sin and heal their land.

Time after time God is recorded as having done exactly what He promised. What appeared as an unavoidable collapse of nations and people groups was suddenly transformed into a revival that changed the spiritual and moral fabric of the culture. Our collective cry in the face of both the sordid conditions facing us and the ancient promises of God ought to be this: "Lord, do it again!"

I will leave the study of revival in history to other books. The story is there for all who will heed: God continually comes through on His promises in repeated times of personal, regional, national and world distress.

## A Prophetic Awakening

Forty years ago I was part of a revival that swept through our church, changing the whole cultural landscape. The result was that thousands of people in our community (by conservative estimate, over two thousand in six months) were saved through the ministries of our local church. One aspect of our experience strikes a parallel to other historical times of revival: The folks saved in the wake of the revival seemed more apt, eager and aggressive than those saved in more "normal" times. I suppose it helps when church congregants are revived prior to a great ingathering of new converts—and ours were revived and ready.

I mention this local church renewal because it was directly related to the Holy Spirit. A few months before this revival, my whole staff was filled with the Holy Spirit. Miss Bertha Smith was a Southern Baptist missionary, long since retired from her beloved mission field of China. After being removed from China to Taiwan and then Formosa, she was deeply grieved at having to leave the northern province of Shantung, China, where a mighty revival had swept through the region. She was further disappointed with her mandatory retirement from her foreign missions appointment at age 65.

Miss Bertha returned to America with a mandate to "cry aloud and spare not and show this people their sins." This amazing woman, whom I met when she was in her eighties (she lived to within months of seeing one hundred years), was invited to minister to the women of the church I pastor. What a spectacle: a little elderly woman standing in a Baptist pulpit, preaching! She would not have called what she was doing preaching, but believe me, it was preaching.

Bertha asked three questions in her presentation: (1) Have you been born again? (It was her conviction that the Church in general was filled with unconverted people.) (2) Have you been filled with the Spirit? (Keep in mind, this question in itself was controversial, as Baptists were widely divided on the question of any such post-conversion experience.) (3) Are you being filled with the Spirit today? (Though she espoused the filling with the Spirit as an experience, she strongly taught that the filling must be continuous.)

Bertha pressed us on all these points with unrelenting zeal. The result of her ministry in only a few days was that a pastor and his staff, and a scattering of his people, were wondrously filled with the Spirit. It is this subject—the proximity of revival

81

to fresh emphasis on the Holy Spirit—that I want to examine in this chapter.

## Confusion of Terms

The religious world—including, unfortunately, the Christian world—uses terms that divide. Yet while we are driven to exclusion and division, God has wider margins than most of us and tends toward inclusion. Religious disagreement is inevitable, but we must not become disagreeable. (Indeed, if we are driven to anger in defending a long and loudly held position, we may be revealing a doubt or two about our own position!) Please, I ask you to allow me the privilege of being wrong, according to your thinking, without closing your hearing to me on a subject over which many are divided.

When we approach the issue of the Holy Spirit, two terms are seen as synonymous: baptism and filling. Charismatics tend to use the phrase "baptism of the Spirit" while most evangelicals shy away from its usage, preferring the term "filling." In the Bible, the phrase "filled with the Spirit" is used far more often than "baptism of the Spirit" but does not weaken the latter's vitality. For the reader's sake, let me say that I believe the "baptism with the Spirit" is an event in which a person or group is filled with the Spirit—while the phrase "filled with the Spirit" refers not only to an event but to a process, something we will discuss later. This simply is to say that there is one baptism and many fillings (or a continuous filling), as we remain "fill-able."

While there is much emphasis today on the baptism of (or with) the Spirit as an event, there seems too little emphasis on an ongoing set of conditions that should flow from the baptism, which involves many subsequent fillings.

Forty years ago, following that revival in our church, I wrote a book on the subject of the Holy Spirit, *The Key to Triumphant Living*. It was my first book, chronicling our revival. I asked Miss Bertha to help me write the book's final chapter, "How

You Can Be Filled Today." She not only gave me help in the details of that chapter, but as we laid the finished manuscript on the floor we got on our knees and prayed it would be given wide reading, intersecting the lives of believers everywhere. The book has met with uncommon receptivity, with more than one million copies in many printed and reprinted formats. Countless people around the world have reported to me that, during a period of reassessment, defeat or transition in their lives, the book's message changed them.

## The Centrality of the Holy Spirit

Not all doctrines are created equal. Widely and deeply differing positions on some doctrines seem to affect the Body of Christ adversely, while others greatly deepen our fellowship and our service to God. I am convinced that what a person believes about the Holy Spirit is the single most powerful determinant of the effect He will have on us.

For years, as I wrote in my testimony, I reacted to what I thought were extremes in the practice of those who believed in the primacy of the Spirit. What I suffered by my own reaction was far more serious than what may have been the effect of wrong doctrines and questionable practices on the other side. I urge you, let my confession widen your consideration for the possibility of needing a shift in your theology.

The Holy Spirit, the Third Person of the Trinity, is the Spirit of God in the world today—and there is no other God. I have said this in another way: The only God on the planet is the Holy Spirit of God, and His presence is the presence of both the Father and His Son, Jesus Christ. Great care should be exercised in dealing with God's Holy Spirit, as He appears to be the one person of the Godhead against whom we cannot sin without disastrous results.

I further offer a reminder that to refuse to deal with the Spirit is to refuse to deal with God, as they are the same. To refuse to deal with the Spirit is also a refusal to deal with Jesus, as they are one as well. I cannot be too emphatic on this, and I grieve to this day that for years I did not understand this powerful violation of spiritual protocol. As a boy preacher I received little instruction or help from any peers, teachers or anyone else. The result? A life and ministry lived on a human level, doing the best I could do. I had experiences of rising and falling in the spiritual life but, had I been honest, I would have reflected that there simply had to be more.

## Time to Get It Straight

My quiet observations of the truths of the Bible about the Holy Spirit forced me to realize that the "more" I needed had to be an issue I had with no one less than the Spirit of God Himself. I knew about Him and believed in Him, but I simply did not trust Him as I had trusted Jesus. He was the Stranger of whom I was afraid, instead of the Living God whom I loved—quite a situation! What would happen when I was filled with the Spirit? Would I lose my church? Possibly so. Would I lose my income? Same possibility. Would I be different, and if so, how different? I wanted to mark off the boundaries prior to getting into this adventure.

I answered these questions with forced honesty, as it happened. Because Miss Bertha spoke the truth about being filled with the Spirit, a collision was inevitable. After several messages from her on the subject of the Holy Spirit, it was decision time—for all of us. Those of us who were convicted gathered in the music room for prayer. There were no more than twenty people, most of whom were staff members and their spouses. Since we were seeking the will of God, happily for us the Spirit came. My associate, who if I remember correctly ended up lying under the grand piano, began weeping and crying aloud, "Oh, God, I want to be filled with the Spirit, and I want to feel it when it happens!" Our music director followed suit and was wonderfully filled.

Amid all this, I was pondering my own situation regarding the Spirit. I had reached a point where I thought I had been filled because I was open to it. I had bowed my proud head some years earlier and surrendered at a new level to the Lordship of Jesus Christ. I had awakened to the fact that this wonderful Lord was alive inside me, my "hope of glory" (Colossians 1:27). But something was still lacking. I was haunted by two deficiencies: the lack of consuming joy and the lack of obvious power in ministry.

A remembered interchange seemed to take place while others around me were being filled with the Spirit. I was having a conversation with God the Father. I prayed, "Father, I thank You for what happened in my life five years ago when I discovered that Jesus was alive in me. But I have noticed a lack of joy and a similar lack of power in my life and ministry." Almost simultaneously with that confession, I distinctly heard what I knew to be the inner voice of God, saying, "Son, what is missing is the Holy Spirit."

I knew what God meant by this. Though I had opened myself to the Spirit, I still feared Him, what He might do and what might happen because of what He did. My proud heart offered one last gasp as my discomfort grew: "But, Father, the Holy Spirit didn't come to talk about Himself."

I was quoting a statement by Jesus in John 16:12–13: "I have much more to say to you, more than you can now bear. But when he, the Spirit of truth, comes, he will guide you into all the truth. He *will not speak on his own*; he will speak only what he hears, and he will tell you what is yet to come" (emphasis mine).

I have capitalized here a statement that I and others in the evangelical faith had used to fend off the necessity of emphasizing the ministry of the Holy Spirit. I had construed it to mean that the Spirit had not come to speak about Himself. It is clear that this was not what was meant in the passage. What it means is that He would not speak apart from what He heard the Father and Son say.

God's reply to my inner being was direct and concise: "My son, you are right that He [the Spirit] did not come to talk about Himself, but I talk about Him, and My Son talked about Him, and My Word talks about Him—and if you and I are going to walk together, you are going to talk about Him."

A deep conviction was aroused in my spirit. For all those years that I allowed fear and tradition to keep me from the Spirit's ministry, I had grieved Him, the only God in the universe. I began to weep out my confession, and soon my weeping was joined by laughter.

Something happened to me that night that was to change my ministry, my life and my church. Had I not studied on the subject of the fullness of the Spirit, I would not have suspected what was happening. As far as I know, it happened to everyone else in the room.

Ultimately, in His faithfulness the Searching Stranger tracked me down and tore the religious mask from my face—and I was exposed before Him. The result was that my whole church was, in a span of three months, plunged into a spiritual transition that made us dizzy with excitement. What was happening could not have originated with us, though we were accused of acting strangely. I remember being visited in a staff meeting by a missionary who had heard of what was happening in our church. Her response to our obvious joy and excitement was, "You all seem to be slaphappy!" Though we did not understand the implications of the term, we joyously took a guilty plea for being "slaphappy."

I have sought across these many years to assess what happened to me in the filling and baptism of the Spirit—and have sought to articulate it in a manner that would prevent many from living deprived as I was for years. Allow me to offer you four observations that apply to this grand adventure of the baptism and filling with the Holy Spirit.

## What Is the Baptism in and Filling with the Holy Spirit?

*One: It is* a fact of Scripture—*and we are obliged to believe it.*

There is no doubt as to the pivotal fact of the filling of the Spirit. The primitive Church experienced it and shared it. In Acts 2, the 120 were gathered under the command of the departed Jesus to "stay in the city until you have been clothed with power from on high" (Luke 24:49). The record reads that when the Day of Pentecost was fully come, they were together in one place, and a sound like a blowing, mighty wind filled the whole place where they were sitting. "They saw what seemed to be tongues of fire that separated and came to rest on each of them [an individual coming]. All of them were filled with the Holy Spirit and began to speak in other tongues as the Spirit enabled them" (Acts 2:3–4). Without a doubt, what Jesus had prophesied had begun to be fulfilled! They were all "filled with the Spirit"—a corporate filling.

Later, as the infant Church began to spring to life with all its expressions, prayer was common and inevitable, and the results were both sudden and remarkable. Words such as "amazed" and "perplexed" are used to describe the watching world, their reactions "bewilderment" and "astonishment."

Obvious shock and concern at these "strange" goings-on were common reactions. Yet so was undeniable boldness by those baptized in the Spirit. Early in Acts 5, two believers who may have been prominent in the Jerusalem church were struck down dead, one right after the other—because, in Peter's words, they had "lied to the Holy Spirit." The reality of God's presence in the person of the Holy Spirit had created a deep sense of seriousness about belonging to the early Church.

At one point Peter was brought in for interrogation by the high priest and his family for having healed a certain man. They asked Peter, "By what power or name did you do this?" The apostle marched through the obviously opened door and began to preach Jesus. Luke reports of the interrogation, "Then Peter, filled with Holy Spirit, said to them . . ." (Acts 4:8). Peter the coward became Peter the conqueror after he was filled with the Spirit.

The apostle Paul both modeled this boldness and commanded it. Acts 9 contains the story of his conversion—the sudden confrontation on the road to Damascus, his being struck blind and led to lodging in the city, his refusing food and water. A certain disciple named Ananias had a divine visitation and received instructions as to where he would find this man from Tarsus in a desperate condition. He was commissioned to lay hands on Paul, saying, "The Lord—Jesus, who appeared to you on the road as you were coming here—has sent me so that you may see again and be filled with the Holy Spirit" (Acts 9:17). There it is again: Just as Peter was filled with the Holy Spirit, Saul was filled with the Spirit. Pivotal in Paul's life, don't you think?

It is no surprise that Paul, when writing his powerful book to the Ephesians, would say,

> Be very careful, then, how you live—not as unwise but as wise, making the most of every opportunity, because the days are evil. Therefore do not be foolish, but understand what the Lord's will is. Do not get drunk on wine, which leads to debauchery. Instead, be filled with the Spirit.
>
> Ephesians 5:15–18

We are not through with Acts, because Dr. Luke, seemingly eager for proper details, mentions the Holy Spirit no less than sixty times in his book. In one passage (Acts 4:24–31) an unspecified number of Jesus' followers were gathered in a prayer meeting. Much of the content of their praying is chronicled:

> "Sovereign Lord," they said, "you made the heavens and the earth and sea, and everything in them. You spoke by the Holy Spirit through the mouth of your servant, our father David: 'Why do the nations rage and the peoples plot in vain? The kings of the

earth rise up and the rulers gather together against the Lord and his anointed one.' Indeed Herod and Pontius Pilate met together with the Gentiles and the people of Israel in this city to conspire against your holy servant Jesus, whom you anointed. They did what your power and will had decided beforehand should happen. Now, Lord, consider their threats and enable your servants to speak your word with great boldness. Stretch out your hand to heal and perform signs and wonders through the name of your holy servant Jesus."

Now, reader, stop and read that passage over again and know that God has heard the reading of those ancient words. What happened then and there can happen here and now right where you are. Are you ready? "After they prayed, the place where they were meeting was shaken. And they were all filled with the Holy Spirit and spoke the word of God boldly."

This is of special note because it records another time—in addition to Pentecost—when there was a group filling. Scripture records additional such events:

All the believers were one in heart and mind.

Acts 4:32a

No one claimed that any of their possessions was his own, but they shared everything they had.

Acts 4:32b

With great power the apostles continued to testify to the resurrection of the Lord Jesus.

Acts 4:33a

And God's grace was so powerfully at work in them all.

Acts 4:33b

If you have any doubt at this point of the importance of the filling of the Spirit and its importance in the life of the believer and the Church, it may be helpful to review some foundational understanding.

Before the birth of Jesus, Zechariah was on duty in the Temple and saw an angel standing at the right side of the altar of incense. Zachariah was understandably "startled and gripped with fear." What the angel said might have settled his fear, but other elevated emotions immediately arose to take fear's place.

> "Do not be afraid, Zechariah; your prayer has been heard. Your wife Elizabeth will bear you a son, and you are to call him John. He will be a joy and delight to you, and many will rejoice because of his birth, for he will be great in the sight of the Lord. He is never to take wine or other fermented drink, and he will *be filled with the Holy Spirit* even before he is born."
>
> Luke 1:13–15, emphasis mine

All of this was too much for poor Zechariah, whose response was an enormous emotional overload. After hearing the astounding message from the angel, he expressed doubt: "How can I be sure of this? I am an old man and my wife is well along in years" (Luke 1:18). In a moment of apparent celestial irritation, the angel said,

> "I am Gabriel. I stand in the presence of God, and I have been sent to speak to you this good news. And now you will be silent and not be able to speak until the day this happens, because you did not believe my words, which will come true at their appointed time."
>
> Luke 1:19–20

This passage is important regarding the ministry of John the Baptist. His destiny was connected with heralding the coming of Jesus as Messiah and the turning of "the hearts of the parents to their children and the disobedient to the wisdom of the righteous—to make ready a people prepared for the Lord" (Luke 1:17). For some nine months, then, Zachariah was quiet, wordless and silent, while the world awaited the appearance of the one who would announce the coming of Jesus and the Kingdom.

It may well have been that what seemed a punishment for Zechariah's unbelief may have protected him from uttering further words that could have undermined the whole process. Whatever the case, it was during Elizabeth's pregnancy that she was visited by Mary, her cousin and the mother-to-be of Jesus. At Mary's salutation, Elizabeth was filled with the Spirit and the babe "leaped" in her womb. It was surely at this moment that the child who would be John the Baptizer was touched by the Holy Spirit. This would fulfill Gabriel's word that John would be filled with the Spirit from his mother's womb. What a chain of events!

As if all this were not enough, when John the Baptist was born, Zechariah's voice was suddenly restored—and in the midst of praising God he was filled with the Spirit and prophesied (Luke 1:67).

While there are other proofs that the filling of the Spirit is a fact of Scripture, it is undeniably and ultimately proven so by the fact that Jesus was filled with the Spirit. It happened very probably, if not certainly, in His mother's womb. Mary was impregnated by the Spirit when the Spirit came upon her, the Most High overshadowing the cosmic event. It may be considered conjecture, but I believe it is a safe conclusion that amid this heavenly episode Mary—the precious teenager designated to be the human agent through which Jesus would make His earthly appearance—was filled with the Spirit. I have no doubt in my mind!

Add to this the fact that Jesus—surely already filled with the Spirit as He lived His years from babyhood to thirty years of age—was formally recognized as God's voice sounded over the baptism scene: "This is my Son, whom I love; with him I am well pleased" (Matthew 3:17). The following chapter in Luke begins with the words, "Jesus, full of the Holy Spirit, left the

Jordan and was led by the Spirit into the wilderness, where for forty days he was tempted by the devil" (Luke 4:1–2).

Is it no surprise, then, that being filled with the Spirit was so pivotal in the early Church and among the believers in Acts, and in all believers throughout history. Our role is not to question this happening or even to understand it but to pursue it.

*Two: The baptism or filling with the Holy Spirit is a revelation—and we are obliged to receive it.*

While it is important that the fullness of the Spirit is a foundational truth of Scripture, it is not enough to merely believe it as a fact. We are not saved by facts, and we will not be filled with the Spirit by merely believing factual information. Somewhere in the process of dealing with facts on the pages of sacred Scripture, the truth must be touched by the Spirit—and transformed into life-changing revelation!

Though we cannot be conclusive regarding the nature of the revelation on the Spirit's filling, we may safely observe that the following will be involved:

- A revelation of the futility of living for and serving God in the flesh
- A revelation of the necessity of being filled with the Spirit
- A revelation of the Lordship of Jesus Christ in the believer's life
- A revelation of the necessity of a total commitment of everything within us to Him

While I knew these things as fact—I would have agreed point by point while nevertheless walking in the flesh—through study and meditation it became suddenly clear to me that there was no viable alternative to being filled with the Spirit. God's mandate to me that strategic evening in 1970 was that unless I did business with the Holy Spirit, allowing Him to fill as well as fix me, I had no reason to believe that I had grounds on which to walk with God.

What was intimated to me on that fateful evening was that until I opened my whole life, fears and all, to His Holy Spirit, I could not expect true peace and joy or, indeed, any facet of the fruit of the Spirit. I could have seasons of human success and some measure of happiness and joy, and in fact for years I enjoyed a measure of these. But as for real spiritual power and effectiveness, the forecast was partly cloudy. There simply was no substitute for being filled with the Spirit.

How do we get this revelation of the primacy of being filled with the Spirit? Read again what you have already read, slowly and distinctly, asking God for light, saying over your life, "Let there be light!" Please know that God is more eager to have you filled with the Spirit *than you could ever be.*

> "Which of you fathers, if your son asks for a fish, will give him a snake instead? Or if he asks for an egg, will give him a scorpion? If you then, though you are evil, know how to give good gifts to your children, how much more will your Father in heaven give the Holy Spirit to those who ask him!"
>
> Luke 11:11–13

Not only is the filling with the Spirit a fact of Scripture to be believed and a revelation from God to be received—it is also an event.

### Three: It is an event—and we are obliged to experience it.

Most evangelicals will find this one issue problematic. Isn't the experience of being saved the ultimate—the whole, the end? Well, if the salvation event is the end, it is the front end, the beginning, the front page, chapter one!

When I was saved on a Tuesday morning of a "revival meeting" in my country church 67 years ago, in my mind I had made the ultimate decision and was quite satisfied. But it was not long before there stirred in my soul such questions as, "What happened? What now? What next?" I would give my life to preach the Gospel but would live many years before getting a hint of the answers to those gnawing questions. Void for years of any working knowledge of the person and work of the Holy Spirit, I had no points of reference that would recommend me to the Spirit's leading, fruit, wisdom and enabling. Is it any wonder that church life without the Spirit is so unsatisfying, incomplete and boring?

Yes, weary saint, there is such a fact as the filling of the Holy Spirit—believe it! It is a revelation—receive it! It is an event—experience it! But it does not stop at being an event—far from it. This Spirit is never static but living, vibrant, exciting and alive with activity. The best is yet to come!

*Four: It is a* relationship—*and we are obliged to continue it.*

Facts may lead to relationships, but they can never substitute for relationships. The vital, boundless sea of truths about God can never satisfy the soul. Yet the Holy Spirit given to us is what makes the whole of the Christian experience a present-tense relationship on both levels of the human journey: the vertical (with God) and the horizontal (our fellow human beings).

Through the ministry of the Spirit of God we are ushered into a relationship with God Himself, and that means we are in relationship with God as Father, God as Son and God as Holy Spirit. We experience Fatherhood through the Father and Sonship through the Son. We experience the flow of life and love through the Holy Spirit for what the ancients called the original Sweet Society: God the Father, God the Son and God the Holy Spirit. We have been inducted into that Sweet Society and are next of kin to God.

Having settled the foundational relationship vertically, we begin to preview heaven by relating in the Spirit to earthlings on a horizontal level. This is no mechanical, legal or imagined level, but is founded and grounded firmly on the promises of Scripture and the continuing necessity to be filled.

## What about Sustainability?

This filling experience is great, but will it last? It is a great mountaintop experience, but what about the waiting valley? The little poem is too true to be very funny:

> To live above with saints we love, now that will be glory!
> To live below with saints we know, now that's another story!

Is it possible to sustain such a life as being filled with the Spirit? The answer is a resounding *YES!* Before you extend the answer to a sad and retiring, "Yes, *but* . . ." let me tell you it is possible also to live and not sin—not *probable* but *possible*. How?

If being filled with the Spirit means we have yielded our lives in their entirety to Jesus, then there are seeds of sustainability in every one of us. As our eyes and hearts are on Him, we are on the road to perfection—and each day we live in Him presents us with more excitement and satisfaction that our end is achievable.

Perhaps there is a man or woman alive who has so experienced God and is being so filled with the Spirit that he or she seldom or never sins. If there is not such a person, I want to be that one. Indeed, if those people exist, I want to be in their company! I cannot live excitedly if I have the assumption that I am surely bound to sin every day of my life. I have Jesus within me by the Spirit of God—and having His nature and inner culture in my inner man, I possess all things that pertain to life and godliness. I am not bound for the Kingdom—I am a full-fledged citizen of the Kingdom, the original Sweet Society, now. I refuse to dwell on the probabilities of repeatedly sinning. I choose instead to dwell on what Jesus has done for me in His dying and is doing for me in His living right now.

As my wife and I partook in Communion recently, I heard myself pray the following, which I had never heard before: "Thank You, Jesus, that when You died for me, You provided everything I will ever need to resolve the sin problem. And as You live in me, You provide everything I will ever need to resolve the self problem." Being filled with the Spirit is God's total answer to man's total need!

Let me recap the four considerations we have examined:

1. The baptism and filling of the Spirit is a *fact of Scripture;* it must be *believed.*
2. The baptism and filling of the Spirit is a *revelation;* it must be *received.*
3. The baptism and filling of the Spirit is an *event;* it must be *experienced.*
4. The baptism and filling of the Sprit is a *relationship;* it must be *continued.*

Listen to a vital voice of the past, that of Charles Haddon Spurgeon, on the subject we have considered:

> Death and condemnation to the church that is not yearning after the Spirit, and crying and groaning until the Spirit is wrought mightily in her midst. He is here; he has never gone back since he descended at Pentecost. He is often grieved and vexed, for he is peculiarly jealous and sensitive; and the one sin never forgiven has to do with his blessed person; therefore let us be tender towards him, walk humbly before him, wait earnestly on him and resolve that there should be nothing knowingly continued that would prevent him from working in our midst.
>
> Brethren, if we do not have the Spirit of God, it would be better to shut the churches, to nail up the doors and put a black cross on them and say, "God have mercy on us!" If you ministers have not the Spirit of God, you had better not preach, and you people had better stay at home. I think I speak not too strongly

when I say that the church in the land without the Spirit of God is rather a curse than a blessing. This is a solemn word: the Holy Spirit or nothing and worse than nothing.

> The Holy Ghost is here,
> Where saints in prayer agree;
> As Jesus' parting gift he's near
> Each pleading company.
>
> Not far away is he,
> To be by prayer brought nigh,
> But here in present majesty
> As in his courts most high.
>
> He dwells within our soul,
> An ever-welcome guest;
> He reigns in absolute control
> As monarch in our breast.
>
> Our bodies are his shrine,
> And he, indwelling Lord;
> All hail, thou Comforter Divine,
> Be evermore adored!
>
> Obedient to thy will,
> We want to feel thy power,
> O Lord of life, our hopes fulfill,
> And bless this hallowed hour.
> C. H. Spurgeon

Consider also the wisdom of another giant of the past, Charles G. Finney:

When Christ commissioned the disciples to go and preach, he told them to wait in Jerusalem until they were "endued with power from on high" (Luke 24:49). This power was, as everyone knows, the baptism of the Holy Spirit poured out on them on the Day of Pentecost. This was indispensable for the success

97

of the ministry. I did not suppose then, nor do I now, that this baptism was simply the power to work miracles. The power to work miracles and the gift of tongues were given as signs to attest the reality of the divine commission. But the baptism itself was a divine purifying, an anointing bestowing on them a divine illumination and filling them with faith, love, peace and power so that their words were made sharp in the hearts of God's enemies, living and powerful like a two-edged sword (Hebrews 4:12).

I have often been surprised and pained that to this day so little stress is laid upon the Baptism of the Holy Spirit as a qualification for preaching Christ to a sinful world. Without this direct teaching of the Holy Spirit, a man will never make much progress in preaching the gospel.

from Memoirs of Rev. Charles G. Finney, 1876

### A Personal Note

As I have recounted these truths and recalled that initial experience of being filled with the Spirit, I have been moved to pray, "Father, as You did it that day, do it again. Fill me afresh, touch me again and empower me to make a difference in my world. Help others to be filled with the Spirit because of me and these words."

I recall the deep and overwhelming conviction that I had unknowingly grieved the Father through my ignorance and fears of His Spirit. Those feelings, thankfully, were followed by great delight as I surrendered in total trust of the Holy Spirit. Our church watched Him move in all of us to purify our relationships, anoint our work of ministry and bring new life to our congregation and our community.

Today I am moved to nostalgia and homesickness for those days and happily reminded of the timelessness of the Spirit of God. Those feelings lead me as I pray, "Fill me now anew, Father. Awaken in me all that has waned or now sleeps. Revive my soul in the refreshing power of Your presence!" He has, He does and He will!

Now Father, touch the reader and may many, because of these pages, be filled with your Spirit for the first time or again. May you, dear reader, find the blessed Spirit of God filling your soul as we continue to learn of the wondrous works of God through His Spirit in the world today. Cry out to Him before you read another word—for a refreshing in His presence and a tsunami of revelation and power for these critical days.

# six

# The Works
# of the Holy Spirit

The Spirit's works are so manifold, so deep in their meaning and so far reaching in their implications that to include them all would involve the creation of a library of too many volumes to print. So, as we talk about the wondrous works of the Spirit of God in this chapter, we must be selective to the theme of this book.

To do this, I will limit our examination to the New Testament works of the Holy Spirit. Before we begin this study, however, we must back up and have a fresh look at the Bible itself as being the most vital work of the Spirit in existence. You may think this claim is a bit overreaching, but consider Paul's words in his charge to young Timothy:

> But as for you, continue in what you have learned and have been convinced of, because you know those from whom you learned it, and how from infancy you have known the Holy Scriptures, which are able to make you wise for salvation through faith in

Christ Jesus. All Scripture is God-breathed and is useful for teaching, rebuking, correcting and training in righteousness, so that the servant of God may be thoroughly equipped for every good work.

2 Timothy 3:14–17

Add to this a passage in Peter's second epistle:

Above all, you must understand that no prophecy of Scripture came about by the prophet's own interpretation of things. For prophecy never had its origin in the human will, but prophets, though human, spoke from God as they were carried along by the Holy Spirit.

2 Peter 1:20–21

There is no doubt here that the Bible is a product of the work of the Holy Spirit. Our colleague R. T. Kendall boldly declares that the Bible is indeed the Holy Spirit's greatest work—and I agree! The Bible, as far as we are concerned, stands alone above all the literature of history as a lingering miracle in three aspects.

First, it is a miracle in *origin*, in that it was "God-breathed" (as translated in the New International Version). In the above passage in 2 Timothy 3, the Greek word used is *theopneustos*, indicating the correct translation as "God breathed."

The Spirit of God is the breath of God. In turn, the Bible is an out-of-this-world book, because it originated with God and may be understood to be a distillation of the very breath of God. This is not mere inspiration, as referred to in elevated emotions in writing a poem or a song or painting a great work of art. It is that work of the Spirit of God upon the minds of men that made their writings of divine revelation. Thus we have the miracle of *inspiration*.

Second, the Bible is a miracle in its *perpetuation*. This is the work of the Spirit of God upon the minds of Scripture translators and the texts themselves that guarantees the arrival of the Bible in every successive generation with the originally intended message intact. It is a miracle also of *preservation*, making the existence of the Bible even more wondrous. The Spirit of God not only gives birth to the Bible by the miracle of *inspiration*— He remains active to protect its integrity and correctness by the miracle of *preservation*. Now we have a double miracle!

But this is not all. There is a miracle to be enjoyed daily by all who approach the Bible to benefit themselves and others. This is the miracle of *illumination*—the influence of the Spirit of God upon the minds of students, teachers and other readers providing inner interpretation, understanding and application of Scriptures. This being true, we must never approach the Bible as a mere book to be read and studied. It must be understood that the Holy Spirit is still on earth shining light through His best creation, the Bible. (I realize this observation overlaps a bit with R. T. Kendall's presentation in earlier chapters. Yet if studied and applied it will set the stage for the demonstration of the Spirit's *power*, as the Word and Spirit are joined together in life and ministry.)

What I am about to say may seem tangential, but I believe it to be both relevant and vital. I want to point out what I have called "the hovering heresy" regarding the Bible. It has to do with the Holy Spirit. The heresy, simply stated, is this: God, for centuries, seemed to talk often and repeatedly but since the compiling of the Bible has seldom if ever spoken as He once did.

Before you protest this severe claim of heresy, look about you. You will find that much of the Church today, while stating the deepest respect for the Bible and defending its credibility to the death, puts little or no emphasis on God's willingness and ability to speak today. Much of this is due to a lack of emphasis on the person and work of the Holy Spirit. In the light of this, please consider the following:

While an unregenerate person may have some understanding of the moral implications of the Bible, that person must still know the God of the Bible through faith in Jesus Christ. The unsaved must not be discouraged from reading the Bible, but they must be reminded it was written to God's children. Thus its highest and deepest meanings remain largely hidden—a family secret, if you will—until revealed from the heart of God through the work of the Holy Spirit to the family members. This is called *illumination.*

Furthermore, it is wise to be reminded that even the saved may read, study and present Bible truths with a purely intellectual understanding of Scripture and little influence of the Holy Spirit. While this may produce expressions of morality, human values and blessings, the highest and deepest life-changing results through the Scriptures come with the Spirit's illuminating power.

Let me sum up: The Bible's very existence is a wondrous work of the Spirit of God; its continued existence through the centuries is due to the continued and repeated work of that same Spirit; and the blessed Spirit of God now aids the reading and research of Scriptures by miraculously illuminating them within and through the believer. That is the threefold miracle of the Book of books.

On the morning I was writing this chapter, I had an experience corresponding to what I have stated here. My wife and I were reading our usual five chapters of the Psalms while I was meditating on the Spirit's work of *illumination.* I was reminded that these words were not just black print on white pages but the distillation of the breath of God—or, to put it another way, *the residue of God's speech*—waiting to come to life again. Immediately, as this thought came, what I was reading took on new life and enlivened my whole being. The glow of that influence within me continues until now.

This threefold miracle of the Bible—*inspiration, preservation* and *illumination*—covers the past, present and future. Though God has spoken in His Word, He still speaks inside us, and will continue to speak inside us, always in agreement with His Book, the Bible.

During a particularly strategic period of my life, I was reading the book of Ezekiel when the Spirit stirred me to read closely chapter 24. In this passage Ezekiel is informed of a coming event in his life:

The word of the LORD came to me: "Son of man, with one blow I am about to take away from you the delight of your eyes. Yet do not lament or weep or shed any tears. Groan quietly; do not mourn for the dead. Keep your turban fastened and your sandals on your feet; do not cover your mustache and beard or eat the customary food of mourners." So I spoke to the people in the morning, and in the evening my wife died. The next morning I did as I had been commanded.

Ezekiel 24:15–18

This is not exactly reading material for quiet times! But to my purpose: In a Bible given to me in 1986, I began reading the story of Ezekiel's experience. Curiously, there were four references to dates on this particular page in that Bible—and each time I read the passage, the Spirit confirmed to me that what I read was a word from God for me. I was certain I was hearing from Him that my wife would die before I died. I was not moved to ask God for His timetable, but the frequency of the reminders increased from 1992 through 1998.

Finally, in 1998, the day of our 45th anniversary together, I was brought to the passage again. At that time my wife was in counseling as a result of a long season of silence (a symptom, we discovered, of what would be diagnosed as bipolar disorder). She had hardly spoken a word for three years. One day around that time, I heard these exact words in response to a request for a word from God: "I want you to prepare to spend the rest of your life without her."

Within two years, my wife was wonderfully healed of bipolar disorder and ended her years of long, painful silence. She also entered the most beautiful period of peace and outlook I had ever known her to experience. Then, early in 2000, she was diagnosed with an advanced stage of melanoma. On January 23, 2001, she was taken to heaven.

I tell you these details of our story to emphasize one thing: The Bible, the prime product of the ministry of the Spirit of God, is a continually interactive book due to the Spirit's ceaseless activity as the same Spirit who initially inspired it. The Bible is God's gift to us, divinely brought from heaven to earth to give light on where we stand and directions for how and where we shall walk (Psalm 119:105).

I am constantly thankful for the Bible, the Spirit's great gift to us. This gratitude explodes with growth whenever I experience the voice of the Spirit of God bringing to me the "saying" Word when I read and study the "said" Word.

### The Gift of Salvation: Compliments of the Holy Spirit

This gift of salvation is called the *new birth*. Jesus said in John 3:3–8:

> Jesus replied, "Very truly I tell you, no one can see the kingdom of God unless they are born again." "How can a man be born when they are old?" Nicodemus asked. "Surely they cannot enter a second time into their mother's womb to be born!" Jesus answered, "Very truly I tell you, no one can enter the kingdom of God unless they are born of water and the Spirit. Flesh gives birth to flesh, but the Spirit gives birth to spirit. You should not be surprised at my saying, 'You must be born again.' The wind blows wherever it pleases. You hear its sound, but you cannot tell where it comes from or where it is going. So it is with everyone born of the Spirit."

We have been given not only a Book but a gift of life—eternal salvation—in the Holy Spirit. The whole salvation proposition is a work of the Trinity: The Father loved us and sent Jesus to be the sacrifice for our sins. Through the Son's obedience to death, our debt was paid completely and forever.

Throughout the processes of the salvation experience, it is a shared project. Our salvation is made complete by the Father's love, the Son's death and the Spirit's life. Jesus had to die because God, as God, could not die. Jesus was both God and man, no less one than the other, and He laid his divine nature aside and died as a human being (albeit perfect in that humanity). But in God's majestic plan, though Jesus died in His humanity—the perfect sacrifice for a perfect work—He was raised from the dead by none other than the Holy Spirit (Romans 8:11).

Within the framework of what Paul calls "so great a salvation" (Hebrews 2:3) are many wondrous works attendant to the gift of salvation. And by receiving the gift of salvation, we receive the gift of the Holy Spirit Himself, who monitors and manages our salvation as we obediently cooperate.

## Works of the Holy Spirit in Our Salvation

The Spirit brings *conviction of sin*, as we read in John 16:7–11:

> But very truly I tell you, it is for your good that I am going away. Unless I go away, the Advocate (Holy Spirit) will not come to you; but if I go, I will send him to you. When he comes, he will prove the world to be in the wrong about sin and righteousness and judgment: about sin, because men do not believe in me; about righteousness, because I am going to the Father, where you can see me no longer; and about judgment, because the prince of this world now stands condemned.

The work of conviction is a wondrous work among the many works of the Spirit. He convicts of the true nature of sin. At the root of the sin nature is unbelief. All who become believers in Jesus Christ do so because they have been convicted that their unbelief calls for a vital experience and relationship with Jesus.

The Spirit also convicts of *righteousness*, holding the unattainable righteousness of Jesus Himself before us. The Spirit shows us that while we are far from righteous in our human nature, "God made him who had no sin to be sin for us, so that

107

in him we might become the righteousness of God" (2 Corinthians 5:21). Only the Spirit can convict of righteousness.

He also convicts us of *judgment*, showing that the prince of this world, the devil, has been judged and poses no credible threat to the Kingdom of God. Without this threefold conviction—of sin, righteousness and judgment—we would not have the foundation of truth on which to stand and the power to walk in triumph. It is the Spirit who guides us into all truth and tells us things to come. John 16:13 says: "But when he, the Spirit of truth, comes, he will guide you into all the truth. He will not speak on his own; he will speak only what he hears, and he will tell you what is yet to come." The Spirit of God is our unerring guide on the trail of truth. We can know theological facts that are helpful, but we cannot receive life-changing truth without Him or apart from Him. He lifts the curtain on the future when we need to know certain things.

He glorifies Jesus by taking what belongs to Jesus and making it ours. John 16:14 says: "He will glorify me because it is from me that he will receive what he will make known to you."

The Spirit is the keeper of the treasury containing all that belongs to Christ and makes it ours. No small thing here! Jesus indicated, "All that belongs to the Father is mine. That is why I said the Spirit will receive from me what he will make known to you" (John 16:15).

### Deliverer from Orphanism

The Spirit delivers from orphanism by the presence of Jesus.

> And I will ask the Father, and he will give you another advocate to help you and be with you forever—the Spirit of truth. The world cannot accept him, because it neither sees him nor knows him. But you know him, for he lives with you and will be in you. *I will not leave you as orphans*; I will come to you. Before long, the world will not see me anymore, but you will see me. Because

I live, you also will live. On that day you will realize that I am
in my Father, and you are in me, and I am in you.

John 14:16–20, emphasis mine

Only the Spirit can reveal to us that Jesus is in the Father, that
we are in Him and that He is in us. All this is happening all the
time and has been since we were introduced to Jesus. A pity
that we have not been told by our leaders; a wonder that now
we know!

These are only a few of the many wondrous works of the
Spirit. I will speak of a few more: Giver of hope, Provider of
peace, Filler with joy, Spreader of love. Paul's prayer is for us
all: "May the God of hope fill you with all joy and peace as you
trust in him, so that you may overflow with hope by the power
of the Holy Spirit" (Romans 15:13).

God uses the Spirit to shed His love in our hearts and thus
gives us hope.

And we boast in the hope of the glory of God. No only so, but
we also glory in our sufferings, because we know that suffering
produces perseverance; perseverance, character; and character,
hope. And hope does not put us to shame, because God's love
has been poured out into our hearts through the Holy Spirit,
who has been given to us.

Romans 5:2–5

## Proof of Sonship and Fatherhood

The Spirit cries out within us that we are the sons of God.

The Spirit you received does not make you slaves, so that you live
in fear again; rather, the Spirit you received brought about your
adoption to sonship. And by him we cry "*Abba*, Father." The
Spirit himself testifies with our spirit that we are God's children.

Romans 8:15–16, emphasis mine

## Helper in Prayer

The Spirit helps us in our weakness and in our praying.

> In the same way, the Spirit helps us in our weakness. We do not know what we ought to pray for, but the Spirit himself intercedes for us through wordless groans. And he who searches our hearts knows the mind of the Spirit, because the Spirit intercedes for God's people in accordance with the will of God.
>
> Romans 8:26–27

## Keeper of the Storehouse

The Spirit has the measure of our inheritance prepared for us.

> What no eye has seen, what no ear has heard, and what no human mind has conceived—the things God has prepared for those who love him—these are the things God has revealed to us by his Spirit. The Spirit searches all things, even the deep things of God.
>
> 1 Corinthians 2:9–10

## Giver of Gifts

The Spirit has wondrous gifts, all of which are available and in us today. These are not just manifestations of human giftedness but supernatural abilities with which to love and serve God and serve needy humanity. These gifts have not ceased and will not through the age of the Church. They remain ever available to every born-again person.

When we live a life filled of the Spirit, the practice of any or all of the gifts is immediately accessible as needed. Imagine these supernatural abilities waiting to be available in any situation. They are listed in 1 Corinthians 12:7–11 and are called "manifestations of the Spirit" (verse 7): wisdom, knowledge, faith, healing, miraculous powers, prophecy, discernment (or "distinguishing between spirits"), tongues, interpretation of tongues. Remember that these are all simply facets of life with God, and that "All these are the work of one and the same Spirit, and he gives them to each one" as He determines (1 Corinthians 12:11).

## A Cluster of Good Fruit (Character)

We are enjoined to recognize the fruit of the Spirit (Galatians 5:22–23). These are character facets as expressed by the Holy Spirit, and are quite impressive—even more so when we realize that by the Spirit they are all within our reach. Again, these are not human characteristics but divine products and expressions of God Himself, through the Holy Spirit. When we are baptized and filled with the Spirit, He is free and active to produce this cluster of fruit in us—all of it!

In the natural bent of human character, certain traits seem more obvious in some people than in others. When it comes to the fruit of the Spirit, however, all people may possess all fruit all of the time. This is impossible without continuing to be filled with the Spirit. To be "filled" suggests control, and when the Spirit is in control He bears His fruit through our lives. What a joyous and wondrous work! This, and this only, is the key to authentic character in the Christian life.

This cluster of fruit contains: love, joy, peace, patience (forbearance), kindness, goodness, faithfulness, gentleness, self-control. These are the results of the Spirit's character, and not just our best desires and intentions!

There are many more wondrous works of the Spirit, but there are two of such importance that I have purposely omitted them here in order to put them under the spotlight in a brief chapter to follow.

## seven

# More Wondrous Works

I have saved this chapter to cover two strategic works of the Holy Spirit for two reasons: (1) these works are persistently neglected, devalued or outright denied by a large segment of the Church; and (2) they are utterly indispensable for the preaching of the complete Gospel and the work of the harvest.

### The Spirit, Our Power Source

I want to speak first of the *power* that the Spirit provides for life and ministry.

The early verses of Acts 1 provide a context. Jesus had risen from death, fully recovered His physical strength and held a very busy schedule, giving instructions to the chosen apostles. It seems He may have shown them a brief, elementary preview of what they were expected to do. Then He became fixed on one theme on which He would speak for forty days. Acts 1:3 gives us this vital information: "After his suffering, [Jesus] presented himself to them and gave many convincing proofs that he was

113

alive. He appeared to them over a period of forty days and spoke about *the kingdom of God*" (emphasis mine).

The subject of the Kingdom was a familiar one to the Jews. For years they had found solace that a kingdom was coming and that the king of this kingdom would set things right. The Jews at last could be safe, sound and satisfied.

So when one of Jesus' disciples raised a question about the Kingdom, it would have sounded completely natural to every Jew within earshot: "*Lord,* are you at this time going to restore the kingdom to Israel?"

Here is the remarkable thing about this question: Something preceded it that had already made the question irrelevant. Jesus had said to the disciples in Acts 1:4: "Do not leave Jerusalem, but wait for the gift my Father promised, which you have heard me speak about. For John baptized with water, but in a few days you will be baptized with the Holy Spirit."

If we apply this passage to the present scene—and the disciple's question about the Kingdom—it explains why Jesus' reply was brief, complete and to the point: "It is not for you to know the times or dates the Father has set by his own authority. But you will receive power when the Holy Spirit comes on you; and you will be my witnesses in Jerusalem, and in all Judea and Samaria, and to the ends of the earth" (Acts 1:7–8).

In a brief series of statements, Jesus was saying, "It is none of your business as to when the Kingdom comes. What is important is that there is business to do in the world on behalf of heaven—business that cannot be done in human strength. The Holy Spirit will come on you and you will receive power to cover the earth with a witness of Me."

They were promised power. Remember, we have defined power as the capacity to generate change—thus, the disciples were to become agents of change.

Abruptly after this, Jesus was taken up from them into heaven, and His followers repaired away to an Upper Room where the Holy Spirit would meet them.

## A Clarifying Parenthesis

I want to connect an earlier event to what would happen in that Upper Room when the wind began to blow powerfully through it. This earlier event is recorded in John 20:19–23. It took place on the evening of Jesus' resurrection, before He reconnected with His disciples.

> On the evening of that first day of the week, when the disciples were together, with the doors locked for fear of the Jewish leaders, Jesus came and stood among them and said, "Peace be with you!" After he said this he showed them his hands and side. The disciples were overjoyed when they saw the Lord. Again Jesus said, "Peace be with you! As the Father has sent me, I am sending you." And with that he breathed on them and said, "Receive the Holy Spirit. If you forgive anyone's sins, their sins are forgiven; if you do not forgive them, they are not forgiven."

What happened here is huge in its implications. Jesus was presenting a prophetic word about what was going to happen very soon. Note that Jesus had come into the room miraculously instead of coming in by the door. He simply appeared and immediately identified Himself by showing them the signs of the crucifixion in His hands and side. He surely had their full attention!

It was no time for a lengthy visit—there would be other times for that. He suddenly and powerfully got to the point. His breathing (or blowing) on the disciples was far more than an illustration. As He blew His breath toward them, He said, "Receive Holy Spirit!" (It is worthy of note that in the original Greek He used no article "the" in the reference. This indicates there was no need to specify since there was only One like Him.)

The very tense in which He is recorded as having spoken this indicates what was about to happen. In the Greek language, the tense Jesus used makes the moment even more significant than we normally might expect. The tense was aorist, which strongly indicates the immediacy of what was being spoken. In fact, it may be accompanied by words that indicate "right now." In short, the disciples were not being informed of something that would happen later—but of something that was happening in that very throbbing moment!

The breath of the risen Jesus was and is the very breath of heaven, the breath of God. Did the disciples understand what was happening? Absolutely not—but they were astoundingly receptive as the risen Christ blew on them and commanded receptivity. There is no doubt in my mind that at that very moment, as He breathed out His own Spirit, they received the Holy Spirit and became born again.

Parenthetically, Thomas was absent during this episode. The other disciples had to tell him about it later. Thomas responded, as most of us would have, "Unless I see the nail marks in his hands and put my finger where the nails were, and put my hand into his side, I will not believe" (John 20:25).

Though we may identify with Thomas's doubts, his skepticism was suddenly and completely blown away in a meeting the next week. Jesus appeared as He had the week before, spoke the word of peace as He had before, then turned and spoke directly to Thomas: "Put your finger here; see my hands. Reach out your hand and put it into my side. Stop doubting and believe" (John 20:27).

In the span of a split second, *doubting* Thomas became a *shouting* Thomas, declaring, *"My Lord and my God!"* He had caught up with the rest of the original disciples in a moment's time. His reward? Jesus said, "Because you have seen me, you have believed; blessed are those who have not seen and yet have believed" (verse 29).

At Pentecost, Thomas and the remaining ten disciples (minus Judas) must have awakened to what had happened to them earlier when Jesus blew on them. As they gathered in the Upper Room with over one hundred other followers, the Eleven were not strangers to the coming of the Spirit. Now they gladly received the Spirit, not only as Indweller but as Empowerer.

## Right Answer to a Wrong Question

Now back to the disciples' question about when the promised Kingdom would come. Jesus' answer was that there was no answer—the secret was set solely under God's authority.

Jesus then presented what would have been their answer had they asked the right question: "You shall receive power. . . ." He was not just accommodating their curiosity but was providing the total answer to the world's total need. You see, they—and we—are the ones who hold the key to power to win the day. We were not left here to do work we could accomplish on our own. The task is larger, much larger, than we are. What Jesus has assigned us to be and do absolutely cannot be done apart from the Holy Spirit—and through Him we will do it.

The promise of Jesus in Luke 24:49 became reality: "I am going to send you what my Father has promised; but stay in the city until you have been clothed with power from on high." The Spirit came then and has never left. He remains available to drive the greatest force on earth: a band of saints baptized in and filled with the Holy Spirit, committed to follow Jesus in changing every heart and culture on the face of the earth.

The raw, life-changing power of the Holy Spirit is the only hope to bring the Church back to its mission and might for the greatest days in history. The Holy Spirit came to clothe us with power. May we determine to settle for nothing less.

## The Spirit, the Key to the Kingdom

Paul did not write a great deal about the Kingdom of God, but there is evidence that he preached it wherever he went. It was a familiar and comfortable subject for him. He was a Kingdom man with a Kingdom message. In Antioch, where he had won a large number of disciples, he revealed the heart of his message to the saints: "We must go through many hardships to enter the kingdom of God" (Acts 14:22).

Paul's recognition of the role of the Spirit in the Kingdom was this: "For the kingdom of God is not a matter of eating and drinking, but of righteousness, peace and joy in the Holy Spirit" (Romans 14:17). This is a strategic verse in understanding the Kingdom of God—what it is, what it is not and whose it is.

Nowhere in the Bible do we have a workable definition of the Kingdom. My opinion on the absence of a definition is that the Kingdom is not defined by words but by the person of the Holy Spirit Himself. The Kingdom is *in* the Holy Spirit. It is obvious, in a general sense, that the Kingdom of God is the rule of God over everything and everybody, everywhere, for all time and eternity. In a more specific sense, the Kingdom of God is the redemptive reign of Jesus Christ through His people on earth. It is both now and not yet, present but not fully realized.

More valuable than a proper definition of the Kingdom of God is our personal discovery of the Kingdom, powerfully declaring it and persistently demonstrating it. These things we do by appropriating the Holy Spirit.

Our colleague, R. T. Kendall, defines the Kingdom as simply the realm of the un-grieved Spirit—and he is right! Descriptions and definitions of the Kingdom may abound, but the most vital observation is that whatever the Kingdom is, it is in the Holy Spirit. While Jesus demonstrated the Kingdom, it was by the power of the indwelling Holy Spirit that He was enabled. All that He did was the work of the Spirit, because the Kingdom is in the Holy Spirit.

Indeed, in the Spirit the Kingdom is everything. It fits into nothing; rather, everything fits into it (or is disqualified and "fits out"). In turn, the Kingdom is not understandable except through the revelation of the Spirit. Surely there is no other work of the Holy Spirit more wondrous than its ongoing influence in, on and through the Kingdom of God. It is the work of the Spirit alone to rule over, reveal and expand the government of God throughout the universe.

The Kingdom cannot be learned like other subjects, such as science, geography or history. The Kingdom is learned only through revelation by the Spirit. It cannot be explained, contained or controlled—thus it is unexplainable, uncontainable and uncontrollable. It is not *taught* as much as it is *caught*—and only through the Spirit can it be caught. It cannot be embraced, explained, applied, pursued or entered without the Spirit of God.

Without the initiation of the Spirit, a person has no interest in spiritual things, including the Kingdom (which is the sum total of all things, spiritual or eternal). The Kingdom is not the leading issue, the prime consideration or the most important thought to be sought—it is the *only* thing, everything, the sum total of all that is. To say that the Kingdom is in the Holy Spirit is to identify the Spirit as the One in whom is *everything!* We may have nothing and have the Kingdom, and thus have everything. We may have everything but the Kingdom, and have nothing at all. All of everything in eternal reality is in the Holy Spirit.

When the days on earth are done—when the shaking takes place so that everything shakable is shaken—only the one unshakable thing, the Kingdom, will remain. Then the wisdom of "receiving a kingdom that cannot be shaken" will be under the spotlight (Hebrews 12:28)—and this Kingdom is in Him, the Spirit of God.

The Kingdom of God is *righteousness*. This means that it is right and just, fair and balanced, eternal and infinite because it is in the Holy Spirit. The psalmist declares, "Your righteousness is like the highest mountains, your justice like the great deep" (Psalm 36:6). "Your throne, O God, will last for ever and ever; a scepter of justice will be the scepter of your kingdom" (Psalm 45:6). "Righteousness goes before him and prepares the way for his steps" (Psalm 85:13).

The Kingdom of God is *peace*. This corresponds to one of the Spirit's best products: Every heart searches for peace, and it is only found in the Kingdom. To seek the Kingdom is to seek for peace. To seek the Kingdom is to find it, and to find the Kingdom is to find peace.

The Kingdom of God is *joy*, consistent with Kingdom produce. In short, all that is needed for abundant life is in the Kingdom, and the Kingdom is in the Holy Spirit. His value and work are nothing short of wondrous as well as indispensable!

### Never without Him

Because of the work of His Spirit, we are never without God, never far from God, never out of His mind. His Spirit calls us, caresses us, crowds us into the victorious vortex of intimacy with God. He is helplessly in love with us, eternally committed to us, totally available to us 24/7. He is the facilitator of our faith, the revealer of our riches in Him, the reminder of our destiny, the magnet drawing us to the safe place of life in the Trinity.

The Holy Spirit is nothing if not personal. His infinite mind is always on us. His infinite power is ever available to us. His errorless will is always open to us.

I awakened on the morning of this writing to an intense desire to return to that place of beginning again—where all He has ever said to me, all He has ever done for me, all He has ever thought of me can be experienced, fathomed, processed and applied AGAIN! To this end, I found in James A. Stewart's book *Heaven's Throne Gift* four reminders that give me a track to run on: "What God claims, I yield. What I yield, God accepts. What God accepts, He fills. What God fills, He uses."

May your own heart as well as mine experience anew the glories of Spirit baptism, Spirit filling, Spirit manifestations and Spirit maintenance. And how may this be? Jesus answers from Luke 11:13: "If you then, though you are evil, know how to give good gifts to your children, how much more will your Father in heaven give the Holy Spirit to those who ask him!"

I borrow this prayer from a hymn:

Come, Holy Spirit, come,
Let thy bright beams arise,
Dispel the darkness from our minds,
And open all our eyes.

Convince of our sins,
Then lead to Jesus' blood
And to our wondering view reveal
The secret love of God.

Show us that loving Man
That rules the courts of bliss,
The Lord of Hosts, the Mighty God,
The eternal Prince of Peace.

'Tis thine to cleanse the heart,
To sanctify the soul,
To pour fresh life in every part
And new create the whole.

Dwell, therefore, in our hearts,
Our minds from bondage free;
Then we shall know, and praise and love,
The Father, Son and thee.

                                    C. H. Spurgeon

## A Prayer You Can Help God Answer

As I close my part of this book, I am moved to pray a prayer for you, the reader. Take a moment, read the prayer and wait. You can now help God in His intention to answer it:

> Father, I pray now for the person who has turned to this page
> to find this prayer waiting to be answered. May this reader be
> assured beyond a doubt that the full prayer is the will of God.
> May the reader right now begin to be filled afresh with the Spirit,
> operate powerfully in the gifts of the Spirit, walk precisely in

obedience to the will of the Spirit, think clearly in the wisdom of the Spirit, experience continuously the guidance of the Spirit, produce constantly the fruit of the Spirit of God and know the depth of the passion of the Spirit.

In Jesus' name, Amen!

In the next and final section of this book, written by Charles Carrin, you will witness the power that results from the proper combination of the Word and the Spirit. One of the most—if not *the* most—glaring deficiencies of the modern expressions of Christianity is the lack of power.

At this point I want to reference an ancient myth that seems appropriate. I give no credibility, of course, to the wild "god stories" of mythology, but taken as an illustration this story seems to capture the message of our book.

### An Ancient Myth—A Modern Parable

Hercules is a well-known figure in Greek mythology. Today his name is used in adjectival form to describe something requiring great strength.

Hercules was one of the lesser figures in the plethora of Grecian gods, all of whom were flawed. He apparently possessed a violent temper, which precipitated his slaughtering of his wife and children. As punishment for this dastardly deed, he was assigned by the superior gods to do several extremely difficult works.

Perhaps the most peculiar and difficult task assigned Hercules was that of cleaning the ox stables of King Augeas. This mythical king had three thousand mythical oxen housed in massive mythical stables. These oxen, as the story goes, were greatly blessed by the gods of Greece: They seemed unaffected by the fact that the stables were never cleaned—a neglect that had continued for thirty years! That task now fell to Hercules. He surely took a look at the mess and thought, "This is not only nasty, it is impossible!" Yet having succeeded in previous impossible tasks, he was not one to give up easily.

As the story goes, there were two powerful rivers, the Alphaeus and Paneaus, flowing near the stables. Hercules, not to be undone by dung, made two openings in the mammoth stables, front and back. By this he joined the rivers together and diverted their course by making a single channel through the stables. The result: The stables were cleansed in a single day.

Is this ancient myth senseless to us? In terms of literal truth, yes. But it is not senseless in that it fits a modern paradigm. The Church today is piled high with the dung of meaningless tradition, with paralyzing mediocrity and with unbiblical ideas, combined with disobedience, pride and greed. In turn, the nutrients of yesterday have become the waste of today. Cherished traditions, of value yesterday, have become empty idols and foul stenches.

Without a doubt the Church needs a drastic cleansing. The pastors and reformers cannot do it alone. Many have tried and many have failed—and the dung piles up still higher! What is the remedy?

Through this world and through the Church flow two mighty rivers: the Word and the Spirit. One (the Spirit) empowers the other (the Word). One (the Word) provides the channel for the powerful flow of the other (the Spirit). Both are necessary, both are vital, but they are incomplete without the other. They are complementary each to the other and mutually interdependent. One (the Spirit) is the force, while the other (the Word) is the course. One is the form (the Word), while the other (the Spirit) is the fullness and flow.

Nations have been changed, the spiritual landscape altered, entire cultures captured by the activation of Word and Spirit joined together. Through the years, records exist of whole regions tapping in to the flow of these mighty rivers and experiencing the power of the awesome combination of God's Spirit and God's Word. At present, however, we seem to be trapped in pitiful parentheses. The rivers seem far away, with the will to effectively join channels weak at best.

This "Word Spirit Power" team believes strongly that if we, the Christian community, could connect these great rivers of Word and Spirit—through humility, repentance and persistent, insistent prayer—a new day would dawn for the Church. There would be a wonderful cleansing, a fresh commissioning and a new authority for the people of God.

Jesus, mightier by infinite measure than the mythical Hercules, waits on us to call upon Him to accomplish this great task. His ultimate design for the Church is no secret. He is committed to "make her holy, cleansing her by the washing with water through the word, and to present her to himself as a radiant church, without stain or wrinkle or any other blemish, but holy and blameless" (Ephesians 5:26–27).

Lord, bring the mighty rivers of Word and Spirit together in our world. Let them flow together in a great tsunami of spiritual power through us, both to cleanse the Church and to empower it to change the cultures of the world!

# PART THREE
# POWER

CHARLES CARRIN

# 8

## My Testimony: Transformed by the Power

But you shall receive power when the Holy Spirit has come upon you.

Acts 1:8

I had been in ordained ministry 27 years at the time the mighty river of the Holy Spirit roared into my life. In a matter of minutes my barn was swept clean. A pristine floor was under my feet. The walls were white. Newness surrounded me. I felt as if my feet were in the barn, my face in glory.

For the first time the Holy Spirit was free to empower the Word that had lain captive in my mind. In that anointing I arrived in Chattanooga, Tennessee, to speak at Central Baptist's Fresh Oil/New Wine Conference. It was early morning when I walked into the hotel lobby and saw two couples I knew rushing toward me. As they approached, one of the wives was suddenly slammed backward to the floor. Her husband crashed a second after her. We had not touched. The other couple saw this happen—and then they also fell.

All four were under the power of the Holy Spirit. I will never forget the expression on the face of the receptionist, a young man from India. He rose on his tiptoes behind the counter, eyes as round as saucers, and stared at the four people seemingly dead in his lobby. His jaw dropped as though he feared a gas leak had killed them. "Don't worry," I assured him, "these people are okay. They are experiencing the love of God."

Later that morning, I went to a local mall and the same thing happened. Two young women who recognized me approached, and as we shook hands one of them dropped under the Spirit's power onto the marble floor. From there I went to a nearby restaurant for lunch and saw a group of young people in a large circular booth waving to me, asking that I join them. As I approached, the Holy Spirit fell on them, too, and they began sliding under the table and into the aisle of the restaurant.

In the afternoon my assistant, David Rhea, and I were walking across a large, un-shaded parking lot when a van screeched to a halt near us. Two women jumped out, rushed toward us and asked, "Will you please pray for us?" Words had hardly left my mouth when both of them crumpled to the pavement. No one caught them and the black asphalt was blistering hot. Yet the location seemingly did not matter to God. The women were caught away into His glory.

All of these things happened before my speaking engagement that afternoon at the conference. My topic was "intercession," and I based my talk on Romans 8:26. As I spoke, the Holy Spirit came on the congregation in an astonishing way. Rows of people dropped behind the pews or in the aisles as the Holy Spirit embraced them.

When I got back to the hotel, I was awed by what had happened that day. God seemed to be no respecter of persons—or of situations. Some of those people met Him in very unexpected (and very public) places—a hotel lobby, a mall, a restaurant, a parking lot. Though some of these did not occur in church, in each case the Kingdom had come in power.

I was puzzling over that fact when there came a knock on the door of my hotel room. When I opened it there stood the young Indian receptionist and his wife. "Will you please pray for us?" he asked urgently, pushing his way into the room. "We want to know Jesus! *Please!* Pray that we will know Jesus!"

Again, the words were barely out of my mouth when the couple was slammed to the floor. I learned later that they were Hindus.

The manifestations of God's power that day was not something I tried to do or was even expecting. I was only a spectator—and was as surprised as those to whom these things happened. Such is the power of God—such is His radical mode!

Jack Taylor had introduced me to the Fresh Oil/New Wine Conference several years before, and it was at that year's session I first met R. T. Kendall. At that time R. T. was pastor at Westminster Chapel in London. We bonded immediately—as had Jack and I when we met at an Atlanta conference in the mid-1980s.

One of the most astonishing facts about that day's events was that for the first thirty years of my ministry I had adamantly preached against the "idiocy" of being "slain in the Spirit." Falling under the power, miracles, healing—all were nonsense to me. My hyper-Calvinism and cessation theology kept me locked in a tight religious box that allowed nothing outside my own control. With that mindset I dismissed such supernatural events as emotional silliness. The transformation I underwent from Word to Spirit to Power was dramatic and painful—but very real.

Beginning with the Holy Spirit's move in the hotel lobby that early morning and continuing through the day, these manifestations had been genuine. Lives were impacted and changed.

People who fall under the power are bowing to the Lordship of Jesus Christ (John 18:6, Acts 9:1–18).

I am aware that such "falling" experiences can easily be faked—as can baptism, Communion, worship, wedding ceremonies, anything else we do. It is also painfully true that people are sometimes shoved to the floor by overzealous ministers. But when people are truly overcome by the Holy Spirit and put into His deep state of tranquility, as were these folks, they invariably rise from the experience greatly blessed. The following letter is an example of what I mean:

> *Dear Pastor Carrin,*
>
> *My husband and I lost our four-year-old daughter in a boating accident. We were Christians but knew nothing of the deeper workings and the healing power of the Holy Spirit. We were both very depressed and angry at God. When you ministered to us, we were "slain in the Spirit" for the first time. The Holy Spirit began a healing work in us that has given us a reason to live and to worship His Holy Name. A hunger for more of God began in us that summer night and, praise God, the hunger has never been satisfied!*
>
> *Since that time, we have received the baptism of the Holy Spirit, and the fruit of the Spirit operates in our lives. Thank you for giving your life to the ministry of people who are hurting. Hopefully, my husband and I will have the opportunity to give to others as you have given of yourself to us. Your ministry has changed our lives. God bless you!*
>
> *Susan Archer,*
> *Birmingham, Alabama*

In the first half of my ministry, such a letter never would have been written to me. That has changed, and power manifestations of the Holy Spirit are now routine in my life and ministry. If God could transform me and confirm His Word with signs and wonders (Mark 16:20), He can do the same for you. Jesus' offer of the Holy Spirit's power is made to everyone who believes— and who allows religious insulation to be removed from his life.

Before going into the theology of these experiences, I need to tell you a little about my background and events that finally climaxed with my receiving the Holy Spirit's empowering. When you better understand my past, you can be encouraged for your future.

## A God Who Does Not Rely on Our Backgrounds

The church I grew up in, in Miami, Florida, during the 1930s, was one of the city's pioneer congregations. This was an "old-line" Primitive Baptist church, which tried desperately to hold to a medieval religious practice. We were not Mennonites, but our traditions were just as unbending and strong. Most men and women sat separately. Sermons were frequently chanted and instrumental music was strictly forbidden.

In 1948 we united with another Primitive Baptist congregation of wonderful but ultra-conservative believers. This church was a little more progressive—instrumental music was permitted—but we focused entirely on ourselves and our Anabaptist ancestry. For us, Kingdom theology was a blank page.

Even so, my salvation experience in that church was a miraculous, life-changing event. It was followed a few months later by a startling daytime vision in which I saw myself preaching. That awesome experience was my "call" to ministry. God never asked me to preach—He simply announced that I would.

My ordination took place the following Christmas Day, in 1949, when a presbytery of four godly men laid hands on me. The church and presbytery did not believe the "laying on of hands" conferred any special gifting or power. To them that method of impartation had ceased with the death of the apostle John. My ordination—though very meaningful to me—was only ceremonial.

131

From 1949 to the present, my sixty-plus years of ministry can be divided into two equal parts: In the first half I never saw a drug addict, alcoholic, suicidal person or anyone with similar problems be miraculously delivered by the power of God. It did not happen, nor did I expect it. Like most pastors, my main concern was being doctrinally correct. Physical or emotional problems were always directed to secular therapy. I had nothing else to offer.

When my own crisis came, and neither doctrine nor secular therapy could help, I was left totally without hope. In an undeniable way I was forced to acknowledge there were big gaps in my theology and my relationship with God. What Jesus taught and what I taught were very different.

As was verified that early morning in the hotel lobby, power-absence is no longer my case. Since my baptism in the Spirit in 1977, I have literally seen thousands of lives impacted and miraculously changed by the Holy Spirit. Significantly, many of those people and I did not even speak the same language. When the power of God is present, language barriers disappear. Would I ever go back to my old ministry of powerless preaching? *Never!*

For three decades I had enjoyed what I thought was a successful pastorate and remained contented in my denomination. Privately, however, I was aware of spiritual dryness that was steadily consuming more and more of my life. In my early years of ministry I had been a fun-loving, sanguine personality who met people easily and loved my work. But the unusual blessings in preaching and the joyous church life of my youth had slowly disappeared.

### The Beginning of Change

At the time of my spiritual renewal, I was serving in a beautiful church in Atlanta. We were in one of the city's prestigious old neighborhoods—Druid Hills—when tragedy struck and I dropped into a "dark night of the soul."

For years I had read about pastors going through this blackness but never imagined how horrendous it was—or that it would ever happen to me. It is not possible to explain such an experience. One must go there for oneself.

There were two distinct aspects to my darkness: It was both physical and spiritual. The physical one involved my wife, when the car in which she was riding was slammed into a telephone pole by a runaway truck. At the time this happened, I was two hundred miles away and knew nothing about the accident. Entering our empty house that night I found a note on the living room floor, instructing me to go to Atlanta's Baptist Hospital.

My wife, Laurie, had thirteen broken bones, a collapsed lung, a brain concussion and so many injuries she could not be moved. It was doubtful she would live. As I stood at her bedside she was unable to move or speak. That was the physical aspect of the wreck.

The spiritual aspect of my dark crisis started a month before the accident. I had a terrifying premonition that such a tragedy was going to happen. It was stalking my wife—seemingly waiting for an opportune moment to seize her. I prayed frantically, begging God not to allow it. I wept. I fasted. Nothing seemed to lessen the terrorizing pressure I felt crushing down on me. Nor did it seem to penetrate what I presumed was God's emotionless sovereignty.

I dared not tell my wife. Like me, Laurie was already wearied with ministry and the long demands on our personal lives. Standing there at her hospital bed, I had feelings that flashed from grief to anger, anger to grief and back again. I was absolutely numb, my mind paralyzed with fear. Her already frail spirit had been overwhelmed with a broken body and a future of incredible suffering.

When the wreck occurred that day, I had been away conducting the funeral of a friend. At the exact moment of the vehicles' impact, I had raised my wrist and looked at my watch's setting—it was noon. My mind strangely "photographed" that moment. Later at the hospital, as I pieced the two events together, the previous month's premonitory warning seemed undeniably true.

Turning away from the bed where my wife lay clinging to life, I walked into the corridor, fell against the wall and gripped my face. My insides were screaming. Prayer seemed futile. I was angry at God, at the truck driver, at my own sense of helplessness and everything around us.

A few minutes later I spoke to Laurie's aunt from a telephone in the hospital. She interrupted me to say, "Charles, God is going to bring something good out of this." I was so angered at her words that I wanted to rip the phone off the wall and throw it down the hall. I thought, *If God cared—or had any capacity to care—He would have done something before the tragedy.* It was too late to look to Him for help. With that thought, my night of darkness began.

For days my wife hung on to life by a thread. Our college-age daughter, Cecile, was living at home and was as devastated as I. We each needed the other and were caught in a whirlpool of mutual dependency and despair. During that time a church friend came to my wife's bedside and said, "Laurie, God could have prevented this if He had wanted to."

That statement—destructive as it was—was in perfect accord with our doctrine. Theologically, our view of God's sovereignty affirmed that He could violate His own covenant of grace at will. He was *sovereign*—and He was answerable to no one. The atonement of Jesus had done nothing to temper His Old Testament ferocity. His love seemed unreal—and unreachable.

On hearing the woman's statement, my wife's last flicker of hope went out. *The accident happened because God wanted it to.* In effect, Laurie thought, He had turned His back on her. Why, she wondered, should she pray now asking Him for mercy when He had already shown what He thought of her?

Unknown to me, Laurie quit praying. She abandoned all hope. Fatalism set in, and in separate ways we faced an agonizing hell.

A spirit of rejection took control of our lives. Unable to help each other, we sank into a pit of black despair.

During that painful time, I thought I heard laughter—taunting, shrieking laughter unlike any I had ever heard before. It was bizarre. Strangely, I could not identify the direction from which it came. My first reaction was that I was losing my mind. Then the laughter changed to words: "You knew this was going to happen!" it said. "You even know the exact moment it happened. You were looking at your watch. But you were powerless to stop it!" More laughter followed.

Nothing in my theological training or years of ministry had prepared me for anything as weird and horrifying as this. It was too unbelievable to share with anybody. While I knew it was real, I also knew no one would believe me.

Though I considered myself a sincere student of Scripture, I had avoided preaching about demonic activity recorded in the Bible. Those verses made me uncomfortable. My remedy for church members' strange behavior was secular therapy. Jesus' statement, "Behold, I give you the authority to trample on serpents and scorpions, and over all the power of the enemy, and nothing shall by any means hurt you" (Luke 10:19), had never been part of my belief system.

A revolution would have to take place inside me before I discovered that 30 percent of Jesus' ministry was spent in direct conflict with unclean spirits.

## Ignoring the Holy Spirit's Messages

The Holy Spirit strangely began bringing old lessons back to mind. These included events when I failed to receive His instruction in the past.

One of these involved my favorite place on Lookout Mountain in the northwest corner of Georgia. Two years before Laurie's wreck, I had been on the mountain on a bright October morning as maple trees were in their full glory. I had parked near the eastern bluff and was standing where I had a one-hundred-mile view of the valley and the Appalachian Mountains in the distance. The scene was incredible, but what really captured my mind were the beautiful maple leaves in my hand. The pink, red and gold seemed to be alive, pulsating with color and vitality. There was no deadness about them.

I had learned a few days earlier that these beautiful colors had been present in the leaves all summer long. That fascinated me. Though the red and gold are not visible in July and August, they are present nonetheless. During summer months, the green chlorophyll overpowers them. When shorter days and cooler nights begin, the chlorophyll fades and the more beautiful colors appear.

Now, after the tragic wreck, the Holy Spirit brought me back mentally to that day on the mountain—and, for an incredible moment, I saw the leaves *spiritually*. It is impossible to explain, but this time I felt I was looking into the leaves—*through* the leaves—*and even felt as if I could see them from the inside out.*

In that instant I understood what Paul meant when he said, "There is a natural body, and there is a spiritual body" (1 Corinthians 15:44). Like the leaves, I knew that I had two identities: summer green and autumn gold. The green represented my visible body and natural life. The gold represented my spiritual person or "hidden man of the heart." The outer man had the power to obscure the spiritual man the same way the green obscured the gold. Somehow I saw the green as being an "insulation" that hindered the Holy Spirit's release of power from my inner person. This obstacle is ego, pride, vanity, conceit, self-centeredness, etc. Religious deception is the most formidable deception of all.

Standing in the hospital corridor now, I recalled something the Holy Spirit had said to me that day on the mountain. It was this: *"Charles, your green has got to go!"* Alone outside of Laurie's room, I knew immediately what the Spirit meant. If I truly wanted to be an authentic New Testament minister, I would die to self and allow Him to come unhindered through me. In that way, the green in my life would be crucified so that the resurrection power of Jesus could pass freely to others.

But another battle followed: How did this fit in with what I believed to be godly Calvinistic teaching? I was convinced that God was sovereign—He did not need my consent to do His will. I found myself rationalizing God's impression on me of the leaves and tried to interpret it through my denominational bias. Within a short time the impression about the leaves was gone.

Strangely, however, a statement from my pastor of thirty years earlier also came back to mind. He had said, "Charles, the church is like the funeral home that puts cosmetics on the corpse. Cosmetics make a dead body look alive when it is not. In the same way, the church can give the impression of having life when it isn't there." I was provoked by this now. I hated to admit it, but there was more death in my past than life. I urgently wanted the Holy Spirit to leave the past alone, to let it stay where it was. But, no, He kept digging into old mental closets and reminding me of lessons He had tried to make me learn sooner.

Along came another. During my early pastorate in Atlanta, I read an article about a local family who owned an antique European mirror. It had hung over their mantle for years, but when the frame came apart they took it down for repair. While restoring it, the repairman discovered a valuable painting by the famous French artist Jean-Baptiste Corot hidden behind the glass. The cover-up had probably been done during wartime to protect it from thieves. When the original owners died, the mirror was sold and knowledge of the painting lost. It would have remained unknown forever had not the frame come apart.

At the time I read the story, I was strangely moved. "Charles," I sensed the Holy Spirit speaking to me, "you read My Word in the same way those people looked in their mirror. They saw only an eighth of an inch deep—nothing more. It wasn't until the frame came apart that they discovered the mirror's true value."

I listened but was at a loss to grasp the message. The Lord was saying this, in essence: "You study the Bible to learn doctrine. But there is truth and power in My Word that you refuse to see. I want you to get beyond the print and encounter Me!"

## A Slow Learner

Did that rebuke—stern as it was—open my eyes to deeper truth in Scripture? No. At that time I was *religiously* devoted to denominational doctrine and did not know how to implement the change—at least, I convinced myself I didn't know. While my brand of Calvinism blinded me, any other "ism" would have had the same effect. Like many pastors, I would not yield until tragedy had smashed my mirror and torn the frame apart.

While I now realize that God did not cause the wreck, I also know that He can in "all things work together for good to those who love [him]" (Romans 8:28). More than that, I belatedly realized He wanted me to get out of my religious foxhole and spiritually journey with Him beyond my own well-built walls. More than anything else He desired that I would experience what Jesus promised Nathaniel: "Most assuredly, I say to you, hereafter you shall see heaven open, and the angels of God ascending and descending upon the Son of Man" (John 1:51). That could happen only if I saw *through* the glass.

What was my reaction to God's entreaty? I continued screaming at Him for new answers. I did not like the old ones; I pushed all reminders of the past away. I only knew one thing: Something very dark and sinister was in control of my family's lives and we were powerless to fight it.

My pastor friends had no explanations for the eerie premonition that had come to pass. Our doctrine simply did not venture into such areas. Theologically, my peers knew what I knew—I knew what they knew—and I knew *we did not know*. As far as I was concerned, no one had the answer.

Physically, spiritually, emotionally, I sank deeper into night-marish depression. I had come to the end of three decades of ministry in a broken pile. For me, life, ministry, everything had ended in total defeat the day my watch read 12:00.

My biggest problem was that I knew nothing about spiritual warfare, including the reality of demons, or the Scriptures' warning against sorcery (Isaiah 47:11–12). In thousands of sermons, I had never devoted one message to the subject of rebuking the devil. On that topic I was a complete blank. Had anyone tried to talk to me about it, I would probably have dismissed the person as a fanatic.

Like many other pastors, I was insulated from learning anything that did not bear the stamp of denominational approval. In my religious egotism, no doctrine could be right if I did not already know it. The fact that I had "authority to trample on serpents and scorpions, and over all the power of the enemy" was unknown territory (Luke 10:19). In this vulnerable state, I was easy prey for powers of darkness. Any idea of being "able to stand against the wiles of the devil" (Ephesians 6:11) was totally foreign to me.

Physically, my wife began to recover. Mentally, neither of us improved. Instead, my depression worsened, moving me steadily toward suicide. This represented a total personality change for me. I had always been a happy, fun-loving person. That abruptly ended.

Forty days after the accident, Laurie was discharged from the hospital. She was confined to a wheelchair for months, however, and could not lift herself out of bed. With her battling constant pain, I could not tell her about the hellish depression that was getting fierce control of me. Yet I did not want sympathy, so no one knew of my crisis. My only desire was to get off of the planet. If God did not do it for me, I would do it for myself.

With that plan hidden deeply in my mind, my world became incredibly black. At night I could not sleep and longed for the day. In the day, that feeling reversed and I longed for the night. One afternoon when I could stand the depression no longer, I got into my car, drove along the Stone Mountain Freeway, floorboarded the accelerator and took both hands off the wheel. Bridges, vehicles and highway signs flashed past me with lightning speed. I have no idea how fast I was driving. Waving both hands in the air I screamed at God, "What are You going to do about it?" The next half hour is a blank. I only know later I was parked in my driveway staring at the hood of the car.

Without telling Laurie, I consulted a doctor who prescribed medication for my depression. Instead of helping, the depression grew severely worse. At my request the doctor changed the prescription and I hurried back to the pharmacist who had filled the original one. When I told him how negatively the medication had affected me, he leaned forward, clinched his hands, fixed his eyes intently on mine and said, "This is the same stuff you've been taking—only it is *twice as strong.*"

"Don't fill it!" I said, and stared unbelievingly back at him. I then walked away, confused and angry at the doctor. Medication was my only hope—there was nothing else—but a doubling of the drug would have put me in a hospital bed.

That night I lay awake, staring into the dark. "God, if You don't kill me I am going to do it for You," I cried. Two hours later I was still awake. Then it was three hours. Four hours passed. Sometime afterward, I collapsed into sleep for what seemed like a few tumultuous minutes. When I awoke my fists were clinched in a tight grip.

## The First Promise of Hope

One of my escapes was to take long walks to a heavily wooded area near our home. My favorite spot was a deep, forested ravine where I could find places to hide. Now, however, I no longer prayed in words but only groans. Soon even this once-sacred place lost its appeal.

One morning I walked in a different direction, turning along a busy thoroughfare. With no forewarning whatsoever, I heard the Lord's voice above the noise of traffic. He clearly said, "Here in the city of Atlanta you will meet your 'Ananias.'"

I was shocked, stopping instantly. The voice had been unmistakably plain. I tried to rationalize this message: "Me? Meet Ananias?" It was puzzling. What did it mean? Saul of Tarsus was blind—I was not. Why would I need an "Ananias"? Saul's being "filled with the Holy Spirit" through the laying on of hands by Ananias never once entered my mind. It was an idea alien to my theology.

Though I should have found encouragement in the message, I did not. But neither could I shake it from me. Not knowing what it meant only depressed me more. As I met new people I would sometimes study them, asking myself, "Could this one be my 'Ananias'?" Yet, the days continued to be dark.

One day I came home from my walk, slumped at my desk and scribbled a few lines. They were prophetic—far beyond my understanding—but I did not connect them to my Ananias, to my denominational box or to my future. I wrote:

> I need to walk new streets today,
> Too long the old have heard my feet;
> My plodding on the worn, familiar way
> Have left me yearning, incomplete—
> So, I seek new streets today.
>
> I need a different world today;
> Old friends in new faces I must find,
> In the unknown mob that crowds my way
> Some strong hand shall grip with mine—
> So, I seek him on new streets today.

# nine

# Ananias: Bringing God's Power into My Life

And Ananias went his way and entered the house; and laying his hands on him he said, "Brother Saul, the Lord Jesus, who appeared to you on the road as you came, has sent me that you may receive your sight and be filled with the Holy Spirit." Immediately there fell from his eyes something like scales, and he received his sight at once; and he arose and was baptized.

Acts 9:17–18

A short time after hearing from the Lord I would meet my "Ananias," a church member dropped in for early morning coffee. This man taught at the Atlanta Federal Penitentiary. He told me, "Charles, I have a prisoner in my class I would like you to meet."

"I'll go some other time," I interrupted. With all the pain I was enduring, I had no inclination to care for prisoners. He looked surprised and puzzled, but he had no idea how eagerly my mind wanted an escape. Then a thought struck me: Being around other traumatized men might help me. The next day I arrived promptly at the penitentiary.

It was then I was introduced to a prisoner I will call Tom. I instantly realized one thing about this young convict: He was the most remarkable Christian I had ever met. From our introduction onward, my attention was riveted to him. There was a calmness and serenity in Tom I had never seen even in my most devout church members. He seemed unaffected by the place's oppressive coldness. A feeling of spiritual darkness permeated the prison, but it did not touch Tom. At times I stared at him, wondering if I was actually detecting a soft glow outlining his body.

Quietly, Tom told me his story. The year before he had attempted suicide by injecting an overdose of heroin. He was an addict and drugs had destroyed his life. There was enough poison in the syringe that day to have killed four men. The needle was in Tom's arm and he was ready to shove it the rest of the way when Jesus spoke to him: "I died that you might live. It isn't necessary that you die also. Trust in Me." The message was that simple. The choice was eternal.

For a moment Tom hesitated. Then, when he jerked the needle out and threw it to the floor, he was born again. Not only that, but he was instantly delivered from addiction and suicide. Cravings never returned. In that same wonderful moment, Tom was filled with the Holy Spirit. A year later, when Tom stepped into my life, he was saturated with Scriptures and the Holy Spirit's anointing.

Looking back, my reaction seems odd. I was magnetically drawn to Tom, desperately wanting what he had—but I was also afraid of him. He quoted Scripture passages about the Holy Spirit that my denomination avoided. He experienced "gifts" of the Spirit, which we claimed no longer existed. Simply put, I wanted what Tom had, but I did not want to change my theology to get it.

I also knew that if I ever experienced what he had, I would lose my church, my home, my income, my friends—everything

I had worked thirty years to achieve. My loss would be great. Yet if I rejected it, there was no other solution to my deepening crisis. One thing was certain: I could not continue to live as I was. Tom talked about the Holy Spirit as if He were his permanent cellmate. Sharing with me about the Spirit's "gifts" seemed to be his joy, his life, his breath—everything important to him.

I was an old-school Baptist, and the spiritual gift that terrified me most was the gift of tongues. I wanted nothing to do with it and told Tom so. Tongues was undignified. Worse still, it seemed mindless and absurd. But the way Tom challenged me with Scriptures left me without defense.

He also had personal "words of knowledge" about me that were too accurate to deny. He even described events that happened to me when I had been miles away. As huge as this penitentiary was, and with no way for him to see outside its massive walls, Tom would sometimes know the moment I arrived and would be waiting for me. It frequently required an hour for me to get clearance and be admitted to the visitors' room, but when I was finally given access I would hear the loudspeaker order him to that area. Security would check me through two huge electric steel gates.

Tom's cellblock was on the left of the gates with a tiny barred window at shoulder height. As I entered the gates one day I heard Tom's name called. I glanced at his window and saw his face pressed against the bars. "Tom," I called to him. "What are you doing?"

"Waiting on you."

"But they just called your name," I answered. "I heard them."

"Charles," he laughed, "the Holy Spirit told me when you drove into the parking lot."

The man literally knocked me back with his amazing knowledge. According to him, all of this information came as a result of his "praying in tongues." He said they were "words of knowledge"—which was both amazing and frightening to me (1 Corinthians 14:2).

When I arrived another time, Tom was working in the prison yard pouring concrete with a team of inmates. Standing in the wet cement, wearing hip boots, he was stirring with a hoe and splattered with ooze. Suddenly he dropped the hoe and spoke to his superintendent, "May I go to the shower and wash up? I have a visitor."

The foreman, a Christian, said, "Tom, they haven't called you to the visitors' room."

"I know, sir, but they will, and it's going to take me a long time to get clean."

"Who is your visitor?"

"Charles."

"Go ahead."

Tom was in the shower when he was summoned to the reception area.

Even though I was awed by these experiences, I shivered at the thought of the gift of tongues and wanted nothing to do with it. I told the Lord so. Sometimes when I prayed at home—kneeling, clutching a bedpost, head bowed—I cried, "Lord, I want to be filled with the Holy Spirit. I need to be filled. My only condition is that I *do not want to speak in tongues.*" Then I would add emphatically, "Nor do I want to shout or be spectacular."

With those conditions uttered, I continued, "You may fill me now—go ahead." Nothing happened. I waited. I prayed again. Nothing happened—absolutely nothing. Sometimes I would keep praying and then waiting expectantly. Finally, I would stand to my feet, puzzled as to why God ignored me. He knew I was sincere and my "no tongues, no shouting, nothing spectacular" request was reasonable. What was going on?

## Scripture Entering My Life in a New Way

One day as I waited for Tom in the visitors' room, I opened the Bible randomly and read Psalm 35:1: "Plead my cause, O

146

LORD, with those who strive with me; fight against those who fight against me."

The passage spoke powerfully to me about my urgent need for help, as I was still plagued by confusion, depression and anger. A moment later I closed the Bible and pushed it to a corner of the table. Tom soon joined me, opened the Bible to the identical passage and said, "Charles, God wants you to hear this." He then gave a profound interpretation of the psalm's message to me personally. I was overwhelmed at his reading the same Scripture I had just read. Moreover, his spiritual insight was beyond my explanation.

The next week when I returned to the prison I was still puzzling over the incident. As I waited, I read Matthew 10:1–8. This passage tells of Jesus sending out the first disciples and enduing them with power to cast out demons and heal the sick. Suddenly, I closed the book. "Lord," I said, "last week when Tom read the same passage back to me, was that coincidence or was that You?" There was anxiousness in my voice as I continued: "If that was You, please, have him do it again." With that, I closed the Bible and pushed it away.

A short time later, Tom entered, took the Bible, turned immediately to Matthew 10 and read the passage. His voice was emphatic: "Charles, God wants you to hear this. He wants you to experience the same power of the Holy Spirit He gave the first disciples." I barely heard what he said. I was astonished at what God had done!

Later, as I left the penitentiary, my head was still swirling from the experience. On the outside steps I stopped abruptly. "Lord," I prayed, "I am grateful for these little signs of Your speaking through Tom. But I want a big one." My brain searched for something suitable to request. "Next week when I come back, I want Tom to tell me that all week long he has been studying the book of Joshua," I prayed, choosing the book randomly. "And, Lord," I added, "I want him to read to me from the first part of the book." My request made, I rushed to the car.

147

When I returned to the prison the following week, I never opened my Bible. Nor would I even think "Joshua." I simply sat waiting for Tom with my mind empty. Tom soon rushed in, and without sitting down he reached over my shoulder and picked up the Bible. "Charles," he said, "all week long God has had me reading in the book of Joshua for you."

I held my breath. He then read to me from chapters one and three. It was as if—in the background—I could hear the Holy Spirit saying, "Do you need *more* proof, Charles? Why do you not believe?" I can still sense Joshua's words washing over me as Tom read them that day: "Have I not commanded you? Be strong and of good courage; do not be afraid, nor be dismayed, for the LORD your God *is* with you wherever you go" (Joshua 1:9).

One would think that such miraculous signs would have immediately blasted me free from my religious stronghold. They did not. Religion can keep a paralyzing grip on its victim. I wanted the "new wine" of the Spirit, but I desperately wanted it in the "old wineskin." Stubbornly—like a man refusing rescue from the Niagara River—I could hear the falls roaring as I got closer. More sleepless nights, horrendous days and hellish depression passed by week after week without my surrendering. One day at the prison, I distinctly heard the Lord say, "Charles, be quiet! Listen to what Tom has to say. He has your answer."

Finally, on Wednesday before Thanksgiving Day, I went to the prison and found myself weeping uncontrollably. My brain was in chaos. Suicidal depression had a stranglehold on me. At least four times I went to the men's room to wash my face and blow my nose. Each time the guard had to unlock the door and let me in. The scene must have been baffling to the inmates and wives who watched from nearby tables. Here I was, a well-dressed pastor who was broken and unable to suppress my grief, seeking help from a convict in olive drab. Our roles were completely reversed. It did not matter: That day I was literally going over the falls and felt the surge of the cataract grab my boat. I determined that when I left the prison that day I would not go home. I would kill myself.

As a man in utter defeat, I suddenly dropped my face down on the table and mentally disappeared into a black hole. There was no more resistance in me. Tom never asked my permission when he laid his hand on my head. His voice sounded as if it came from light years away when he said, "Brother Charles, 'The Lord Jesus, who appeared to you on the road as you came, has sent me that you may receive your sight and be filled with the Holy Spirit'" (Acts 9:17). Those were Ananias' exact words to Saul of Tarsus.

Surrounded as we were by some of the nation's top gangsters and criminals, the room became my "house on the street called Straight" (verse 11). In a moment's time, it was transformed into a new city of Damascus.

When I arrived home, I sprawled across the bed with my suit still on. It was then the Holy Spirit invaded the room with a glory that goes beyond all earthly explanation. There is no vocabulary to describe the power that raced through my body. I was exorcized of a demon of depression and suicide. In a moment's time, every death wish was gone. Depression was jerked out of me like roots snatched from the ground. More than that, my body was bathed—*caressed*—in oceans of incredible love.

I next felt myself being baptized in the Holy Spirit. It was an experience of going into the Spirit as the Spirit came into me. Instead of going over Niagara Falls, I felt like I was standing under the falls and the Holy Spirit—like the water in the cataract—was pouring into me. He filled each crevice and fissure while He healed every wound in my being. Mental injuries that went all the way back to childhood felt His healing touch. I have to paraphrase several old hymns to describe the Holy Spirit's wonderful presence:

Earth receded—it disappeared—
Heaven opened on my eyes,
My ears with sounds angelic rang.[1]

1. From "Vital Spark of Heavenly Flame" by Alexander Pope, 1712.

There I bathed my weary soul
In seas of heavenly rest,
And not a wave of trouble rolled
Across my peaceful breast.[2]

Heaven came down my soul to greet,
And glory crowned the Mercy Seat![3]

All of these words had suddenly come true for me. How long the *Presence* was upon me I don't know. Like Israel with Moses, I was baptized in the "cloud and in the sea" at the same time (1 Corinthians 10:2). Time and space lost their meaning. "Whether in the body or out of the body I do not know" (2 Corinthians 12:3). I am certain that I did not move, but it seemed that my body lifted from the bed and became suspended in space. I was weightless, with no sense of gravity touching me.

Best of all, my "dark night of the soul" had ended forever. Weeping had endured for a night, but joy had finally come in the morning (Psalm 30:5). Strangely, it was not until that moment that I recognized Tom's identity: There in the Atlanta Federal Penitentiary I had met my "Ananias." He was Tom. God had kept the promise He made to me that painful day on the sidewalk.

### Tom and I: A Future Together?

In the months that followed, my relationship with Tom intensified. We planned to minister together as soon as he was released from prison. I was his only contact with the outside world, and he was my only contact with the spiritual world. In the truest sense we became soul brothers and eagerly looked forward to the future.

My visits to the prison were like holidays to him and banquets to me. We both relished the time to talk about our heavenly

2. From "When I Can Read My Title Clear" by Isaac Watts, 1707.
3. From "From Every Stormy Wind That Blows" by Hugh Stowell, c. 1865.

Friend. Whereas that visitors' room had witnessed my intense grief and Tom's deep concern, it now witnessed our joy and laughter. One day when we were at our table excitedly discussing our future, the Holy Spirit suddenly interrupted and spoke simultaneously to both of us. The words were unmistakable—but they were terrifying. The expression in Tom's eyes told me he had heard exactly what I heard. I heard what he had heard. The message was too distinct—too precise—to misunderstand. In a commanding voice the Holy Spirit said, *"Tell each other good-bye."*

I stared at Tom incredulously. He fixed his eyes, wide with grief, at me. Several moments passed as we sat unmoving. Then, as if in a rehearsed plan, we rose, hugged each other, said good-bye and in separate directions walked out of the room. I did not look back. I couldn't. I heard a heavy metal door slam shut behind him. That was the last time we ever saw each other.

I left the building never to return. In more than thirty years since, I have not once tried to find Tom. My life became very public—sometimes international—but Tom never made any effort to contact me, either. We had said good-bye at the Lord's urging, and we had known deep down it was good-bye forever.

At the time I did not challenge God's command. I endured a long, painful wait before I understood His reason. God knew that Tom and I would have been two vines leaning on each other. To that possibility, the Holy Spirit said, "No." He did not want me depending on Tom, or Tom depending on me. Our dependence had to be each of us trusting wholly on the Lord. God wanted us separately to become oaks—we could not be vines together.

It was much later that I realized Tom's five-digit prison ID number began with the numbers "888." In Scripture, "8" is the numeral representing new beginnings. Even more significant to me was that "888" is the Greek numerical value of all the letters in Jesus' name.

## Lasting Effects

The long-range effects of my deliverance and baptism were phenomenal. For two years, I never read a newspaper, watched TV, listened to radio or sang a secular song. Discipline was unnecessary. I wanted nothing to interfere with my love for Jesus. Old attitudes changed; others disappeared totally, never to return.

Denominational errors that had controlled me from youth vanished. Suddenly I knew that Jesus still healed. Like it or not, I knew the gift of tongues was God's method for crucifying ego, vanity and religious intellectualism. While I was more motivated to love the Church than I had ever been, I saw the greater reality of the Kingdom of God. It was superlative: The Kingdom was all-encompassing. Somehow I sensed a power unknown before that was lying just below the surface of my being. What would release it, I did not know. But it was there.

My theology was transformed in dramatic ways. The Bible was the same, but new truths seemed to leap off the page at me. I could now look through the glass. While I had preached constantly about the Church and very little about the Kingdom, I discovered that Jesus spoke of the Church only three times (Matthew 16:18; 18:17), but He spoke of the "Kingdom" some 130 times. I could not find the word *church* in Mark, Luke or John—it was not there. Jesus loved the Church and gave Himself for her—and so must we—but His focus was on the Kingdom.

One statement stood out above the rest. Jesus said, "If I cast out demons by the Spirit of God, surely the *kingdom* of God has come upon you" (Matthew 12:28, emphasis mine). That had happened to me. The Kingdom had come, the demon of depression was gone forever and I was free. Suddenly I wanted to free others from every form of demonic oppression. And, in fact, spiritual gifts began manifesting in me almost immediately after my baptism in the Spirit, and I ministered in the Spirit's power.

God's renewal in me was not finished, however. Six weeks after my baptism in the Spirit, around 3 A.M., I was asleep, dreaming that I was reclining on an open-air porch with my arm resting on a banister. Suddenly, the dream changed to a vision. An incredibly beautiful dove, white and glistening, flew from behind my head and suspended itself above my wrist. Its feathers, beak and every detail of its body were as distinct as if they had been etched in porcelain by a jeweler's tool. Each feature was perfect.

The dove shimmered with brilliant light. In its beak was a tiny, purse-like object. I remember saying, "Isn't this amazing? The dove is not afraid of me!" In that instant, the dove landed on my wrist and turned into a sunburst of blinding, silver light. Immediately in the dream, my body was blasted with what seemed like ten million volts of electricity. My only conscious thought was that I was dead—electrocuted. No one could survive such a jolt. The dove disappeared, but when I woke my body was still vibrating violently on the bed.

Nothing in my past—experientially or theologically—had prepared me for this. I had no knowledge as to what it meant. Nor could I tell of it to anyone. It was too sacred, too incredible. No one would believe me. It was not until years later that I shared the experience with trusted friends, and they interpreted its meaning to me. John the Baptist said of Jesus, "He will baptize you with the Holy Spirit and with fire" (Matthew 3:11). Could this have been the "fire"? I still don't know for sure.

There was yet another phase in God's renewal of me for His service. I have said that the spiritual gifts began manifesting in me almost immediately after my baptism in the Spirit. The one exception was the gift of tongues. This gift remained elusive. At first it was not a concern, but after two years of waiting I found myself agonizing, groaning, yearning for the gift to burst free in me. At times I lay curled on my office floor weeping for its release. Without it I felt incomplete.

Slowly, the facts dawned on me. I had ridiculed this spiritual gift more than any other. I had cautioned my congregation to avoid people who claimed to speak in tongues. "They are not your friends," I warned, "they are enemies. Stay away from them!" Now here I was, weeping for the very thing I had exhorted others to avoid. More repentance followed. Just when I thought I had reached the bottom of my penitence I plunged deeper.

Finally, one day it came. In a single half-hour period, some seven different languages poured out of me. The experience was astonishing. I had studied Greek, Spanish and French in college and I recognized language patterns. Though these new sounds were unidentifiable to me, I knew they were authentic and real. As I had expected, after this gift was released in me, the other gifts began to flow ever more powerfully and freely.

### God Remembering My Carnal Prayer

After my spiritual baptism, I immediately began to preach about the Holy Spirit—but in ways that did not frighten my congregation or arouse suspicion that I had become a threat. If I could, I wanted our church to make the wonderful transition that had come to me. In most sermons I emphasized that "All Scripture [not part] is given by inspiration of God, and is profitable for doctrine" (2 Timothy 3:16).

I was serving new Bible food on denominational plates. Several weeks later at our Sunday evening service, I concluded my sixth sermon about the Spirit's miraculous works. When the service ended I went to the door to greet the people as they left the building. It never occurred to me that the Holy Spirit had an unfinished issue with my demanding "no tongues, no shouting" baptism.

I stood smiling, waiting at the door as two men approached me, extending their hands. I reached out mine—but we never touched. Instead, a shout loud enough to be heard a block away came roaring out of me: "We need God!" I yelled at the top of my lungs. And then as if no one heard me, the shout came out again—*and again.* Three times my voice shook the building, "*We need God! We need God! We need God!*"

The men froze in their tracks, staring wide-eyed at me. Then, pale-faced, they turned and ran back down the aisle toward the exit door. Suddenly, there was a clamor as everyone in the building stampeded that way. I saw my wife running with them.

That shout did not come out of me—and yet it did. The truth is I did not know where it came from. Yes, it was my voice—it had to be. But I would never have done such a thing!

Suddenly, my whole being began swirling. I felt that I was being lifted up to the ceiling—then, no, I was passing downward through the floor. What was happening, I did not know. Fortunately, the rack that held our Gospel tracts was close enough that I grabbed it and held on. My body could not support me—and I did not know where my legs had gone.

A moment later, I felt arms around me as a middle-aged man grabbed me and hugged tightly, giving me loving support. I was too weak to hug him back. This brother was the only person in the building who understood that the Holy Spirit was involved in what was going on with me. Thankfully, he held me up. If I had fallen to the floor, the deacons would have called 911.

Then, as quickly as the shouts had come, my weakness was gone. There was not a trace of heavy breathing or lightness in my head. It was as if it had never happened. But I was embarrassed and did not want to face the people. Special visitors were there that night who had planned to take my wife and me to dinner. But I was humiliated and could hardly face them.

My humiliation turned to anger—at God. When I finally got home, my brief nighttime prayer revealed my ire: "Lord!" I shouted. "This is what I was afraid of! This is the reason I told You I didn't want to shout. I can never feel safe in the pulpit again. Everybody knows Pentecostals are crazy. Now I am, too!"

That night I would not pray. I was so angered, so humiliated, that I would not speak to the One who caused it. A few days passed before I heard the Lord's voice again. Almost casually, He broke into my routine saying, "You need to learn that from

155

now on, I will make the decisions. You don't need to tell Me what you will and will not do." The shouting never happened again.

At that point, I knew nothing about the weird sounds and power demonstrations that occurred in the ministry of Jonathan Edwards, George Whitefield and others. Learning about these things brought a little comfort. Then I read about the Holy Spirit's noisy presence at the Cane Ridge Revival in Kentucky in 1802 and its effect on pioneer America. Somehow my religious education had missed those facts. Nor had I learned about similarly strange things happening in the ministry of John Wesley, Peter Waldo, Alexander Campbell, Augustine, the Puritans, early Baptists, Methodists, Quakers and numerous others throughout Christian history.

The greatest discovery I made was this: *Truth was in the Scriptures, power was in the truth, the Holy Spirit was in the power.* That realization took me into another spiritual dimension. Only as I looked back at my personal history did events in my confused past begin to make sense.

Finally, on the matter of tongues:

## Ego: A Monster of Opposition

The glory that had invaded me that bleak November day when Tom laid hands on me in the prison was producing unusual results. I was yet to learn that ego and pride were the biggest handicaps to anointed ministry—and that they usually disappear only at a slow rate.

Jesus said, "You will receive power when the Holy Spirit comes upon you"—and it happened! He came, I received and the power rushed in (Acts 1:8). The next challenge for me was to remove the spiritual insulation so the power was free to come out. During that time I wrote these lines about myself:

> Of all the things that die,
> Ego dies the hardest;

156

There is no heart arrest—
No sudden stopping of the breath,
Just a slow and painful grieving
As ego feels its power leaving,
Struggling against the dreaded cross,
Wrongly thinking death is loss,
But—if and when—it dies in grief
How welcome is that sweet relief!

Soon I began to recognize the ego problem in Old and New Testament characters—as well as in myself. My greatest opponent was the one within me: personal ambition, vanity, pride, self-centeredness. If left unchecked, ego would be the great destroyer of opportunity and the dead end of anointing in my new work.

Ego prevents the Holy Spirit's free movement in both the Church and individual believers. God's problem is not getting the power in us as much as getting the power out of us. Many believers have received spiritual gifts that are inactive in them because they are heavily insulated by their carnality. Jesus said, "For everyone who asks receives" (Luke 11:10)—that is Kingdom truth. It is also obviously true, however, that the power of the Spirit is not ministering out of all who possess the gift.

Spiritual gifts are frequently communicated person to person when ego has been crucified. This has been the pattern in Scripture: Moses to Joshua, Elijah to Elisha, Ananias to Paul, Paul to Timothy, Timothy to others, Tom to me, me to you, you to someone else. The impartation goes on independently of the organized Church. This person-to-person ministry is a Kingdom identity. It is undoubtedly what Paul meant when he wrote to the Christians in Rome, "For I long to see you, that I may impart to you some spiritual gift, so that you may be established" (Romans 1:11).

Paul's impartation was not mere instruction, which he could have included in the letter. He had to be present for the gifting to take place, through the laying on of hands. He said to Timothy, "Stir up the gift of God which is in you through the laying on of my hands" (2 Timothy 1:6). You see, our bodies are temples of the Holy Spirit. There is a transfer of power through the hand only when it is an unhindered extension of the temple. In other words, the power is transferred from temple to temple—not just body to body.

However it is explained, I only know that when Prisoner Number 888 finally stepped into my dark night of the soul and laid hands on me, I received an impartation that would continue its movement for decades to come. I would learn, too, that Jesus' statement, "Give and it will be given to you," applied in this context. The more we give to others what God has given us, the more we get. "He who believes in Me," Jesus said, "out of his heart will flow rivers of living water" (John 7:38).

Much later I was reading in Deuteronomy 28:66–67 when my eyes fell on these startling words:

> Your life shall hang in doubt before you; you shall fear day and night, and have no assurance of life. In the morning you shall say, "Oh, that it were evening!" And at evening you shall say, "Oh, that it were morning!" because of the fear which terrifies your heart.

These lines perfectly described my experience. I had been under the curse of the law. Since the curse was broken now and the demon of depression cast out, my "dark night of the soul" had ended forever.

Sometime later, I woke one morning lying where I could see my hand beside me on the bed. My fist was clinched tightly. "Charles!" I said to myself. "You don't have to sleep that way anymore. Open your fist." I still remember that wonderful moment of stretching out my fingers on the sheet and letting them relax.

## Miraculous Gifts Appearing in Ministry

Only a few weeks after my spiritual renewal, I was in my office when a call came from a grief-stricken mother and father in

Augusta, Georgia. Their teenage daughter had run away from home. They had no idea where she had gone but thought Atlanta might be the place. Someone had given them my name as a possible source of help. I reminded them that Atlanta was a city of several million and that finding the girl accidentally was hopeless. God would have to find her for us. We each agreed to pray.

After hanging up the phone I sat at my desk, meditating and asking the Lord for guidance. Suddenly, the name of a hippie bar in the Tenth Street district popped into mind. I had never seen the place but knew it was a gathering spot for runaways and derelict people. "Call them," the inner voice said and then dictated a message to me to give to the bar owner.

A moment later I had an employee of the bar on the phone. "Will you please put a note on your bulletin board for me?" I asked. The note I dictated gave the girl's name and these words to her: "You don't have to come home, but please call. Mom and Dad." The parents' full names were at the bottom.

Two hours later, I was still in my office when the mother called back. "She telephoned us!" she shouted in my ear. "Our daughter went into the bar just minutes after they posted your note. She saw her name and knew we had no way of knowing where she was. She knew God was pursuing her! Thank you, Pastor, thank you!"

The mother broke into uncontrollable weeping. Two Sundays later, all three family members—the mother, father and daughter—were in our Sunday morning worship. Their home was restored.

What happened that day? The Holy Spirit gave a specific "word of knowledge" about the girl's location. Such a "word" is one of the spiritual gifts listed in 1 Corinthians 12. The Lord knew where she was hiding when no one else could have found her.

I realized this word of knowledge was identical to the kind my friend Tom in prison had experienced. Had the Holy Spirit placed onto me the same mantle that had been on Tom? I did not know—but the possibility was exciting. The truth began dawning brightly: Christians who reject the Holy Spirit's miraculous gifts do not realize how severely they handicap their own lives. When pastors scorn the gifts, the tragedy is even worse, for the effect spreads to many. Human wisdom and intellect are not enough for authentic ministry. The Spirit can save us from much ineffective and wasted effort.

Another woman telephoned who had been an alcoholic for eighteen years. She had lost everything. Her husband had divorced her, her children avoided her and her grandchildren were growing up without knowing her. She was well known as the "neighborhood drunk." The basic acts of combing her hair, wearing clean clothes and caring for her appearance were things she ignored. I had once been her pastor, but as a cessation theologian I had been unable to help her. My solution for such problems was to recommend secular therapy. I had nothing else to offer.

But that wonderful day when she called, we took part in a ten-minute, Spirit-led telephone deliverance—and the woman was completely set free. Why? *I had received the power Jesus promised.* He said, "And these signs will follow those who believe: In My name they will cast out demons" (Mark 16:17). On the authority of that promise, the demon of addiction was cast out. Alcohol never bothered that woman again. Not only that, but she was filled with the Holy Spirit and flooded with joy.

For the first time in years, her life was normal. Excitedly, she went back to her church and told people about the Holy Spirit freeing her. The alcoholism was gone—she was a new woman! She anticipated how thrilled everyone would be to hear her good news.

But her testimony frightened them. The pastor—a cessationist—had no theological explanation for her miraculous "deliverance." Nor did he want to learn. Such an experience was not itemized in their denomination's "Articles of Faith."

As cessationists they simply did not want to talk about such things. Sadly, the woman's church friends began avoiding her.

The frightening truth is this: The church could accept her alcoholism because it did not challenge their theology. But they would not accept her deliverance because it dangerously disproved their cessation theory. In effect, they were willing to let her—and others like her—drown in addiction before they would question their denominational doctrine.

In time, the woman was forced to leave the church, where she had been a member for 25 years. Thankfully, she found another congregation that rejoiced in her Holy Spirit rescue. To her dying day, she lived a happy, fruitful, *sober* life.

After taking part in her deliverance that day, I discovered that the experience would be typical of my new ministry. Amazingly, the negative reaction of her church only motivated me to love those people more. I wanted them to experience everything the Holy Spirit had done for me—and for their alcoholic member. Indeed, my experience of Kingdom power fortified my love for local churches, in addition to my own congregation, and enabled me to better serve them.

This fact became supremely clear: The Holy Spirit demanded that I fully accept my "Kingdom identity." This meant acknowledging I was part of the Body of Christ worldwide and not to limit my ministry to a denomination. Denominationalism was now dead forever to me. I could no longer focus on fragments of the Church.

At the same time, my ministry to our local congregation was enhanced because I saw the Church as an extension of the greater Kingdom. That revelation was significant. It was as if I had been admiring the beauty of a single star when suddenly the universe exploded with millions before me. Most importantly, I finally understood that the primary mission of the Church was to reveal the Kingdom and her glorious Messiah-King. Kingdom power was to accompany and authenticate the preaching of the Kingdom.

## Personal Care from the Holy Spirit

My new friend, the Holy Spirit, began showing me how His gifts would care for me in more personal ways.

For years I had escorted tour groups to the Middle East, visiting Israel and other places of Christian interest. The responsibility for caring for large numbers of people in warring areas was sometimes frightening. Once I led a group on a cruise ship that traveled to key sites in the eastern Mediterranean. On this particular trip, we were retracing the missionary journeys of Paul and visiting the locations of the seven churches of Asia.

We were trying to get ashore at Dikili, Turkey, to visit the ruins of Ephesus but were prevented from doing so by a storm at sea. The ship could not get into harbor because of low tides and dangerous waves. Small boats were used to transport passengers ashore—but there was no gangplank. Passengers had to step directly from one ship onto the other. This made the transition hazardous as the two vessels rose and fell independently of each other.

When my turn came, I miscalculated the step and fell about three feet, landing on my knees with my elbows in another man's lap. I was not harmed and we both laughed. When I learned he was an American, I asked which state he was from. "Georgia," he answered.

"I live in Georgia!" I replied in amazement. "Where in Georgia do you live?"

"Atlanta," he continued.

"I'm from Atlanta!" I half-shouted. "Where do you work in Atlanta?"

"I'm a pastor."

By this time, I could hardly believe my ears. "I'm a pastor, too," I answered. "Where is your church?"

He was in the process of answering, "Ponce de Leon Avenue and Oakdale Road," when I interrupted: "My church is at Ponce de Leon Avenue and Oakdale Road!"

There were only two churches at that intersection: mine and a Lutheran congregation, the one where this man was pastor. My office was on the second floor, and every day from my window I had admired the pastor's imposing granite building.

When we both recovered from shock he said to me, "I think the Lord wants you to know that no matter where you go—anywhere in the world—He can have someone there to help you."

He was right. The Holy Spirit is our "paraclete"—the One who travels beside us to give guidance and direction. Thank God! That experience was to become typical of my future.

## The Holy Spirit: Protector and Provider

In spite of my best efforts to educate our congregation, it became known that I no longer fit the denominational pattern. Soon bitter criticisms arose in the church. My next instruction from the Lord was to resign as pastor. I understood His reasons. The people would never deviate from denominational standards, and I could never again be a "denominational" preacher.

I obeyed, resigning, but I completed my tenure through the end of summer. During that time, a pastor drove across the state to accuse me face-to-face of heresy and of deviating from denominational doctrine. Scripture was not the test—traditional doctrine was. Another party who wanted to destroy my credibility brought threats. I went to pray in my hideout, a wooded ravine near our house.

No sooner had I climbed down the slope than I heard the name "Ahithophel!" shouted loudly in my ear. Whether the voice was internal or external I could not tell, but it was so audible it seemed to echo through the woods. I knew God had spoken it. But I had never heard the name before and was afraid I would forget it before I got home.

I ran all the way, saying, "Ahithophel, Ahithophel, Ahithophel. . . ." Rushing to my desk, I grabbed my Bible concordance and found the name in Scripture. When I read the passage I was stunned. Ahithophel was part of a revolt to overthrow King David. The rebellion was led by David's son Absalom (2 Samuel 17:23). Ahithophel's attempt failed, and in time both he and Absalom were killed.

My mind was in a swirl. God had spoken a name totally unknown to me. From that point on, I knew if I relied on the Holy Spirit He would protect me from attackers. More importantly, I saw a new power by the Spirit in the written Word. The Holy Spirit had used a Bible name unknown to me to bring assurance of His protection.

My biggest problem in leaving the church was that my wife and I had no place to go, no savings and no income. Churches where I had preached in the past were now suspicious of me and refused to let me in their pulpits. Most of my pastor friends disappeared. Word quickly spread about my heretical "baptism" in the Spirit. It was whispered that I had lost my mind. The shouting incident provided fuel for that.

Overnight I found myself abandoned. Whereas previously I had been an appreciated minister, edited the denominational magazine, written for its Bible study literature and chaired numerous committees, I was instantly ostracized. My wife and I faced fierce rejection. Even so, as soon as I had fulfilled my commitment, we moved out of the church's spacious parsonage and into a small apartment. We stored most of our furniture in a friend's warehouse, from which it was quickly stolen.

Soon I realized that nonessentials were being systematically stripped from my life. At the same time, the Holy Spirit began demonstrating the power of His anointing. I didn't have to ask, He just did it. Numerous hurting people, like the alcoholic woman, were set free. Supernaturally received messages, similar to the "Ahithophel" and hippie bar experiences, became common. I was given knowledge of future events and walked in a totally new dimension of Spirit-led power. Families were rescued from ruin and physical bodies were healed. It seemed that God had "set before me an open door" of ministry (Revelation 3:8).

At times in worship meetings that I was invited to lead, whether formal or informal, the Holy Spirit invaded like a storm. Hundreds of people were felled by the power of the Spirit and rested in the glory. Some who came only as spectators found themselves acknowledging the Lordship of Jesus. Others were invisibly pinned to the floor and could not be lifted up. One woman was stuck to the wall.

Why such demonstrations? I don't know. Scripture does not give us a list of first-century "signs and wonders." We only know they happened then and are happening now. Are these signs radical? Yes, and they were meant to be. As the modern Church becomes more radical in its unbelief, the Holy Spirit will become more radical in His signs and wonders.

An atheist college professor was slammed to the carpet in one meeting. He came up sobbing, saved and crying, "I found God! I found God!" A paralytic who could not stand without two assistants was healed. Minutes afterward, she went leaping up the center aisle of the church, across the back aisle and down the side. She then raced home to tell her husband. I baptized a young man in the ocean whose body seemed electrified, vibrating uncontrollably as he sank to the bottom numerous times and emerged praying ecstatically in tongues.

A Catholic monsignor experienced deliverance and was filled with the Holy Spirit. He was so amazed by the changes in his life that he arranged for me to speak twice to the faculty and student body of St. Vincent de Paul Catholic Seminary. Young Latin priests suddenly had their eyes opened to the truth of the Gospel and swarmed around me after the meeting. They wanted to know more about the Holy Spirit.

Dave Calyn, a cameraman at the Toronto Airport Fellowship, was literally blown off his platform backward and saw his feet flash on the TV screen before him. A man who had fallen ten feet from a roof, shattering his ankle, was healed—with X-rays to prove it. Another man, who had fragmented his pelvis while roller-skating on a concrete floor and could not walk normally, was healed instantly. Many others have been delivered from addictions or demonic oppression and thousands filled with the Holy Spirit. "Signs and wonders," as Jesus promised? Yes! Can I explain them? No! Are they real? Absolutely! Did miraculous events end with the apostolic age? Absolutely not! For those who choose to believe Scripture, miracles continue to this day.

Soon after my return to Florida, I received a frantic call late one night from the parents of a teenage boy who was undergoing a horrendous demonic attack. The boy was out of his mind and having to be forcibly restrained by three men. When I arrived, the yard was already filled with police cars and fire trucks. After receiving ministry in the power of the Holy Spirit, the youth walked out of the room, completely normal and free. The police officers returned to their station and reported that they had witnessed a "successful exorcism." The *National Enquirer* and other tabloids discovered the story and published it nationwide. Christian publications kept a deathly silence. Why the difference? Most of the current Church does not want to acknowledge that Jesus' power to cast out demons is still there.

An officer with the West Palm Beach, Florida, police department once attended a service where I spoke. Sgt. Larry Castelli, a believer who had not been in church in ten years, had never been in a meeting where the Holy Spirit moved visibly. He was the police department's thirteen-year S.W.A.T. director, a martial arts expert, rappel master, undercover agent, bodybuilder and former marine. This man had rappelled headfirst from high-rise buildings, dropped down elevator shafts and faced violent killers.

Sgt. Castelli and I met before the service began. Then, midway through my sermon, I felt a distinct urging of the Holy Spirit to call him forward. He was surprised to hear his name spoken publicly and did not want to respond. His obedience was slow in coming. As I laid hands on him, a surge of electric-like power went through his body. That was followed by an intense pounding of his heart. He was alarmed and thought he was having a heart attack. Suddenly, he felt his body being pulled downward to the floor. "No!" he said to himself. "You are strong. You are not going to fall—not in front of all these people"—but he did.

As the congregation watched, the Holy Spirit overrode the sergeant's human strength and reduced him to a powerless, humble man. He was on the floor for more than twenty minutes—a submission in which he physically acknowledged the Lordship of Jesus Christ. While in that state and stripped of all human resistance—like Saul of Tarsus—Sgt. Castelli was filled with the Holy Spirit. His life was radically changed. Later, he told how he experienced the greatest love for Jesus he had ever known. Within two years Larry was out of the police force, to which he had been devoted, and he became my personal assistant. Today, he travels with me, helping me in the gifts and power of the Holy Spirit. Such is the mightiness of God!

A psychotherapist called my office and asked if I would minister to eight of her most deeply troubled patients. I reluctantly agreed, thinking this was beyond my depth, and was driven to my knees because I had no experience in dealing with such problems. The Holy Spirit responded with specific instructions. In a short time, all of the patients were totally restored or their conditions improved dramatically. Referring to a particular client, the therapist told me, "I had that person for two years with no improvement. You had her for two weeks and she is normal. Will you teach me? I am giving up my practice and want to do what you are doing."

Rick Cross was a deacon in a Florida church who suffered from crippling arthritis in both hands. He had received the maximum 64 cortisone shots in his knuckles. There was no further medical help available to him, and he had not improved. Then, in a brief two-minute prayer, Rick was totally healed. Ten years later, the arthritis has not returned. Rick now ministers with me, laying those same hands on others for healing.

While ministering to a woman once, I had a "word of knowledge" that she had a spirit of harlotry. I obeyed Jesus' instruction to cast out the spirit, and the woman was successfully delivered.

167

Later she wrote to me: "As a child I was sexually abused by a friend of the family and then by a friend of my brother's. It started at age seven and lasted for a number of years. . . . Today, I am free! Really free! I have been healed physically and spiritually. I feel like a little girl again, so giddy and happy! Praise God, my spiritual growth has been amazing."

A mother wrote me, "I brought my seventeen-year-old daughter to you for prayer. As a child she was labeled 'learning disabled' and was afflicted with epilepsy, migraines and numerous other things. She has not had one seizure or one migraine since you prayed for her. It truly is a miracle. It was the beginning of a restored life for her."

A medical doctor wrote, "Both my hands were healed of pain and weakness that had bothered me for seven or eight years, sometimes hurting all day and night. During your group deliverance, I felt a tremendous pressure rise up through my chest that just disappeared with a big sigh."

A pastor suffering from chronic burnout and suicidal depression came from out of state for help. After his successful deliverance and baptism in the Holy Spirit, he told our ministry team he had a gun in his car. He said, "If this ministry had failed, I was not going home alive." Thankfully, he returned to his church and family a restored man—and renewed as a pastor for Spirit-empowered ministry.

Speaking as a long-term pastor, the most important thing I can tell you is this: I know what it is like to work with—and without—the Holy Spirit's anointing. The old cannot compare with the new. As real as plugging into an electrical outlet, the Spirit will confirm His amazing presence in you. Religion will be replaced with authentic *spirituality and power.*

There are key lessons that helped my change come about. I want to share some of those lessons with you—lessons that connected my ministry to the Holy Spirit's power. As you read, pray that you will see "through the glass" and discover the awesome realities hidden in God's Word. Your ego and pride will begin to melt away, and spiritual gifts that have been obscured in your life will appear in all their beauty. Your "green leaf" will change into red and gold as you step into miraculous ministry. Remember this: *Truth is in the Word. Power is in the truth. The Holy Spirit is in the power.* All of it is waiting for you.

## ten

# Theology
# of the Anointing

When He had been baptized, Jesus came up immediately from the water; and behold, the heavens were opened to Him, and He saw the Spirit of God descending like a dove and alighting upon Him. And suddenly a voice came from heaven, saying, "This is My beloved Son, in whom I am well pleased."

Matthew 3:16–17

Had Herod succeeded in killing Jesus at age two, the Savior's blood would have been just as efficacious for the redemption of humankind as it was 31 years later. As an infant, conceived by the Holy Spirit, Jesus was fully the Son of God when Mary gave birth to Him. Death by Herod's sword or the Roman cross would have made no difference in the merits of His blood. But an additional work of the Holy Spirit was necessary before the *benefit* of Jesus' death could be applied to humankind.

This point is absolutely vital to everyone who desires to minister in the power of the Holy Spirit. If you try to bypass this scriptural fact, you will advance no further in your pursuit of the "demonstration of the Spirit and of power" (1 Corinthians 2:4).

The killing of the Passover lamb and placing its blood in the basin did not save Israel (Exodus 12:21). The blood had to be applied to the doorpost of each Israelite being delivered. Without the application of the blood, Israel's firstborn would have died along with the Egyptians'. The same is true for us: The blood of Jesus must be applied personally to every believer. *This fact necessitated the Holy Spirit's second work in Jesus.* I am referring to the *anointing* that came upon Him in the Jordan and empowered His preaching ministry.

Prior to the Spirit's dove-like descent at His baptism, Jesus healed no one, performed no miracle, preached no gospel of the Kingdom. That abruptly changed when the Holy Spirit's anointing came upon Him. I repeat: Jesus was the Son of God from the moment of the Holy Spirit's conception—and He later became the Messiah, in the Jordan. The word *messiah* is the Hebrew word for "anointed one." In Greek, it is *christos*. The conceptive work of the Spirit destined Jesus to the cross and the work of redemption. It was the messianic anointing that made it possible for the news of redemption to be carried miraculously to the ends of the earth.

In every capacity, Jesus intended the Church—like Himself—to operate in the power of the Holy Spirit. If we try to preach the Gospel of the Kingdom without the anointing, we will experience failure in many vital areas. If Jesus depended on the Holy Spirit, how can we succeed with less?

Jesus' conception by the Spirit was for the purpose of His incarnation and redemption. He was "Emmanuel," "God with us," and heaven's final Passover Lamb. This work of embodying Himself in human flesh climaxed at the cross, when the debt of sin was fully paid and the provision of redemption finalized.

That work is complete and decisive. In that awesome moment—suspended between heaven and earth—the Lord shouted a message from the cross that echoed to the edge of the universe:

"It is finished!" And so it was! The result of the Atonement cannot be magnified or diminished.

What *can* be diminished is the measure of our ministerial success. Anointing and ministry are inseparably connected. This work cannot be finalized until "this gospel of the kingdom will be preached in all the world as a witness to all the nations, and then the end will come" (Matthew 24:14).

Jesus explained in the synagogue of Nazareth that the anointing on Him was to "heal the brokenhearted, to proclaim liberty to the captives, and recovery of sight to the blind, to set at liberty those who are oppressed" (Luke 4:18). To be thorough students of the Word, we must make this distinction carefully. These two works of the Spirit in Jesus' experience—conception and anointing—are distinctive; one cannot replace the other. Both were essential for the completion of redemption. As I have mentioned, prior to His anointing, Jesus preached no Gospel, healed no sickness, performed no miracle. When the anointing came, that inactivity decisively changed.

In His first sermon in Nazareth, Jesus explained, "The Spirit of the LORD is upon Me, because He has anointed Me to preach the gospel to the poor" (Luke 4:18). There is no true Gospel apart from the anointing. This empowered Good News is God's tool for transferring the blood from the basin to the doorposts of humankind. Jesus told the disciples, "As the Father has sent Me, I also send you" (John 20:21). The same Holy Spirit who anointed Jesus would anoint the disciples.

In duplication of Jesus' ministry, the Gospel preached by the first disciples was accompanied by "signs and wonders" and miraculous "gifts of the Holy Spirit." While I have great appreciation for theological seminaries and Bible schools—and for my own training as well—I say without hesitation that institutions cannot impart the anointing. They provide wonderful education, but anointing? No. Without the Holy Spirit's anointing on the preached Word, it remains only inept religious talk. With the anointing, the same message becomes an instrument of awesome, divine power. The presence or absence of the Holy Spirit makes the difference.

## No Substitute for the Anointing

Not only did the Holy Spirit anoint Jesus in the Jordan, but in the same way at Pentecost the Holy Spirit anointed the second Body of Christ, the Church (1 Corinthians 12:27). Jesus' specific instruction to the disciples was to "wait for the Promise of the Father. . . . You shall be baptized with the Holy Spirit not many days from now. . . . You shall receive power when the Holy Spirit has come upon you" (Acts 1:4–5, 8).

The disciples were born again before Pentecost (John 20:22) and that work of the Holy Spirit in them was complete. Yet they had not been anointed by the Holy Spirit for miraculous ministry and evangelizing the world. Without the anointing of God's power upon them individually and corporately, the Gospel could not be presented to the "ends of the earth."

Please hear me carefully: The Holy Spirit's provision for getting the blood miraculously "out of the basin" and onto the people occurred in two distinct events: (1) the anointing of Jesus in the Jordan, and (2) the anointing of the disciples in the Upper Room. Without the anointing, there can be no miraculous attestation of the Gospel. We have seen this verified in the ministry of Jesus and the early Church.

Let me note, too, that the anointing may rest separately on a follower of Jesus or on the Word itself. Jesus said, "The words that I speak to you are spirit, and they are life" (John 6:63). This means that even when His words are conveyed on paper—through a Christian tract or a Bible in a hotel room—they carry the potential of anointing.

In ratifying the Old Covenant, Moses sprinkled both the book and the people with the blood of calves and goats (Hebrews 9:19). In contrast, the New Covenant was ratified by the sprinkling of the blood of Christ (Hebrews 10:29; 12:24). If the Old

Covenant was made inalterably holy by the sprinkling of animal blood, how dare we claim that the New Covenant—sanctified by the blood of Christ Himself—contains passages that are invalid and fallible! I refer specifically to those claims made by some denominations that the gifts of the Spirit, as outlined in 1 Corinthians 12–14, are spurious and should be ignored.

The morning I walked into the hotel lobby and people fell under the power of the Spirit, the anointing was on me as a disciple. It was not on my word, because I was not speaking. When Peter walked the streets of Jerusalem and people were healed by the presence of his shadow (Acts 5:15), the anointing was on him physically. There is no power in a shadow, but the proximity of Peter's body (the Holy Spirit's temple) projected the anointing to those nearby.

The words "Christ" and "Christian"—from the Greek word *chrios*—are not designations of the new birth but of the *anointing*. I share this fact only for the sake of scriptural accuracy. Information about the Gospel may be learned academically, but the actual power of the Gospel can be rendered *only by the unction of the Holy Spirit.*

For this reason Jesus warned the disciples not to depart from Jerusalem but to wait for the promise of the Father. He said, "You shall receive power when the Holy Spirit has come upon you" (Acts 1:5–8). Only after receiving this power could they become witnesses to the "end of the earth."

## The Error of Cessation Theology

To absolve itself of power failure, the contemporary Church has invented an escape hatch called cessation theology. This pleasant-sounding expression declares that God has withdrawn the Holy Spirit's miraculous power from the Church. It says the Church's power is in a book—the Bible—and nowhere else. This doctrine also says if we have no power it is because God has removed it, that the fault is not ours. (Yet, astonishingly, the Lord did not cause Satan's power to be removed at the same time ours supposedly was.)

The apostle Jude did not believe the cessation claim. Instead, he presented one of the New Testament's strongest defenses for the Gospel's inalterability. He said, "I found it necessary to write to you exhorting you to contend earnestly for the faith which was once for all delivered to the saints" (Jude 3).

The phrase "once for all" in this verse comes from a valuable little Greek word, *hapax*. In spite of its brief length, *hapax* carries significant authority. It means "one, a single time, conclusively, absolutely all, every one." This expression appears at least eight times in the Greek New Testament. In the New King James Version it is translated as "once for all" five times. The New International Version translates it as "once" three additional times.

In every instance, *hapax* establishes the un-changeability of its subject. Six of the eight references to *hapax* below apply directly to Jesus, while one applies to the believer and one other to Kingdom faith. In four instances in the Greek text, the preposition *epi* ("upon") is added, to reinforce the "once for all" meaning. Here are the eight *hapax* passages:

1. Romans 6:10. "For the death that [Jesus] died, He died to sin once for all; but the life that He lives, He lives to God."
2. Hebrews 7:27. "Who does not need daily, as those high priests, to offer up sacrifices, first for His own sins and then for the people's, for this He did once for all when He offered up Himself."
3. Hebrews 9:12. "Not with the blood of goats and calves, but with His own blood [Jesus] entered the Most Holy Place once for all, having obtained eternal redemption."
4. Hebrews 9:26. "He then would have had to suffer often since the foundation of the world; but now, once at the end of the ages, He has appeared to put away sin by the sacrifice of Himself."

5. Hebrews 10:2. "For the worshipers, once purified, would have had no more consciousness of sins."
6. Hebrews 10:10. "By that will we have been sanctified through the offering of the body of Jesus Christ once for all."
7. 1 Peter 3:18. "For Christ also suffered once for sins, the just for the unjust, that He might bring us to God, being put to death in the flesh but made alive by the Spirit."
8. Jude 3. "Beloved . . . I found it necessary to write to you exhorting you to contend earnestly for the faith which was once for all delivered to the saints."

After studying these *hapax* ("once for all") passages carefully, to which of them are you willing to apply cessation theology? Read the list again, asking the question once more. Would your theology be complete if any of these "once for all" references were removed from the work of Jesus? Or, are you genuinely glad that they are "once for all" secure? If your answer is the latter, then it is impossible for you to endorse cessation theology. You cannot accept the works of Jesus as *hapax* and also deny the works of the Holy Spirit as *hapax* in the permanency of Scripture. You cannot do it and maintain integrity with God's Word!

Modern Christianity has convinced itself that Jesus provided two distinct Gospels and two distinct faiths—one for the first-century Church and one for the Church that followed after. Cessationists say the first Church was miraculously empowered while the second was not; the first had the baptismal gift of the Holy Spirit, while the second was merely given a book telling what the Holy Spirit had achieved in the past. Hear the truth: Jesus provided everyone—past, present, future—with a faith that was *hapax*-true, *hapax*-strong, *hapax*-forever.

Whether you and I accept it or not, the original "faith which was once for all delivered to the saints" is still intact. It is unaltered. In a conclusive, unchangeable way, the faith of the

177

apostolic era was delivered for "all time" intact to every subsequent generation. There will never be another.

Someone may argue, "But I have never seen the miraculous works of the Holy Spirit in my church!" If that's true, does the fault lie with God or with the church? The contemporary Church is a victim of its own unbelief. It has created its blighted condition. The apostle Jude said he found it "necessary" to "exhort you" to "contend earnestly" for the faith.

Jesus reinforced this truth when He said to the disciples,

> Go therefore and make disciples of all the nations, baptizing them in the name of the Father and of the Son and of the Holy Spirit, teaching them to observe all things that I have commanded you; and lo, I am with you always, even to the end of the age.
>
> Matthew 28:19–20

Jesus was emphatic. His instruction to "teach them all things"—referring specifically to the Church at the "end of the age"—is unmistakably clear. He expected the 21st-century Church to be taught precisely what He taught the first-century Church. There is no such thing as an apostolic Church and a post-apostolic Church. There is simply the Church with "one Lord, one faith, one baptism" (Ephesians 4:5). We can either believe Jesus or men's doctrines of denial. We cannot believe both.

The obvious message is that the Gospel—and the faith arising from it—have been permanently given one time and will never be given again. That initial provision is sufficient "once for all" time and "once for all" people. In an emphatic way, this says that New Testament faith—doctrinally and experientially—as it was originally presented by the Holy Spirit is unchangeable. It cannot be added to or taken from. Any cessation claim that teaches otherwise is a hoax. Such an accusation insults the cross and the work of the Holy Spirit (2 Peter 1:21).

Even so, there is an idea rampant in modern Christianity that parts of the covenant book that Jesus ratified by the sprinkling of His blood have lost validity. This supposedly occurred at the death of the apostle John in A.D. 70, or when the New Testament books were canonized into the authorized Bible in A.D. 367.

To justify the absence of miracles and acquit itself of failure, the modern Church has blamed God for the power's disappearance. But consider what Paul said about such a change:

> I marvel that you are turning away so soon from Him who called you in the grace of Christ, to a different gospel, which is not another; but there are some who trouble you, and want to pervert the gospel of Christ. *But even if we, or an angel from heaven, preach any other gospel to you than what we have preached to you, let him be accursed. As we have said before, so now I say again, if anyone preaches any other gospel to you than what you have received, let him be accursed.*
>
> Galatians 1:6–9, emphasis mine

How could Paul have stated this any plainer? Quoting Paul, I will be so bold as to say that any "gospel" claiming to be different from the original is a humanized gospel. Scripture severely warns against our preaching "another gospel." In the sight of God there is only one: the original Gospel of the Kingdom presented by His Son.

### Spiritual Gifts: Commanded by the Lord

Saul encountered Jesus on the Damascus Road and was born again. Three days later, through the laying on of hands by Ananias, Saul encountered the Holy Spirit and received the Spirit's baptism. Now known as the apostle Paul, he later wrote an 84-verse treatise on spiritual gifts (1 Corinthians 12, 13, 14). His biblical explanation provides the most comprehensive, authoritative information we have on the subject. More important, it is the only resource bearing the seal of divine authorship. All conflicting opinions, no matter how cherished or long established,

179

are but human speculation and must be discarded. Scripture is our final, absolute authority.

Paul begins his dissertation with this plea: "Now concerning spiritual gifts, brethren, I do not want you to be ignorant" (12:1). Interestingly, this appeal that we "not be ignorant" appears seven times in the New Testament concerning different topics. Once it is written by Peter and six times by Paul. Each time, the request reveals an especially deep concern of the writer. Its appearance here should command the attention of every conscientious believer.

Paul then proceeds carefully to detail the operation of nine "grace works" of the Spirit. These are the direct result of the Spirit's baptism. Having defended the need and purpose of the gifts, Paul concludes his discourse with the stirring rebuke, "But if anyone is ignorant, let him be ignorant" (14:38). In other words: "After this careful explanation of spiritual gifts, if anyone refuses to learn, I have nothing more to say to him. Let him remain illiterate!"

Paul seemingly anticipated that some believers would reject his teaching on the miraculous works of the Spirit. He added this harsh warning: "If anyone thinks himself to be a prophet or spiritual, let him acknowledge that the things which I write to you are the commandments of the Lord" (1 Corinthians 14:37).

What are the "commandments" of which Paul speaks? They are the apostolic teachings on spiritual gifts. First Corinthians 12 and 14 speak with God's authority as much as any other of Paul's writings. We are no more at liberty to reject these biblically mandated instructions than any commandment of the Lord.

Until recent years, there was probably no other subject about which the Church was more ignorant than that of spiritual gifts. Instead of heeding Paul's instruction, the Church engaged in open warfare against them. This was done in full view of Paul's exhortation that we (1) "earnestly desire the best gifts" (1 Corinthians 12:31); (2) "pursue love, and desire spiritual gifts, but especially that you may prophesy" (14:1); and (3) "even so you, since you are zealous for spiritual gifts, let it be for the edification of the church that you seek to excel" (14:12).

These admonitions do not indicate the reluctance that typifies the modern Church's attitude against spiritual gifts. There was no such lukewarmness on the part of Paul or the Corinthians. Similarly, believers today are encouraged to exercise the gifts for the benefit of everyone:

> But the manifestation of the Spirit is given to each one for the profit of all; for to one is given the word of wisdom through the Spirit, to another the word of knowledge through the same Spirit, to another faith by the same Spirit, to another gifts of healings by the same Spirit, to another the working of miracles, to another prophecy, to another discerning of spirits, to another different kinds of tongues, to another the interpretation of tongues. But one and the same Spirit works all these things, distributing to each one individually as He wills. . . . But if anyone is ignorant, let him be ignorant.
>
> 1 Corinthians 12:7–11; 14:38

For some the argument immediately arises, "These gifts passed away." Paul did not believe this, nor does the New Testament teach it. In the introduction of his Corinthian letters (29 chapters and the longest of all New Testament writings), Paul exhorted believers to "come short in no gift, eagerly waiting for the revelation of our Lord Jesus Christ" (1 Corinthians 1:7). In this brief statement, Paul equates the duration of spiritual gifts with the length of time the Church will wait for Jesus' return. Examine it for yourself. Even so, there is probably no greater ignorance in the Church today than of spiritual gifts and Jesus' offer—no, His command—for believers to be baptized in the Holy Spirit.

There was no greater day in history than the day in which Jesus ascended. On that special day Jesus told the disciples gathered at the Mount of Olives, "John truly baptized with water, but you shall be baptized with the Holy Spirit not many days from now. . . . But you shall receive power when the Holy Spirit has come upon you" (Acts 1:5, 8).

In a single statement, Jesus connected baptism in the Spirit to the imparting of His power. That wonderful event occurred on the Day of Pentecost, when 120 disciples in the Upper Room received the blessing. Scripture carefully explains that others who were not present at Pentecost experienced the same empowering later. This included the Samaritans (Acts 8:14–17), Saul of Tarsus (Acts 9:17), the household of Cornelius (Acts 10:44) and the Ephesians (Acts 19:1–7). Young Timothy also followed the example (2 Timothy 1:6). Identically today, multiple millions around the world have stepped into the Spirit's wondrous baptism.

### The Argument against the Gift of Tongues

> But whether there are prophecies, they will fail; whether there are tongues, they will cease; whether there is knowledge, it will vanish away. For we know in part and we prophesy in part. But when that which is perfect has come, then that which is in part will be done away.
>
> 1 Corinthians 13:8–10

Those who oppose gifts of the Spirit frequently quote this passage to defend their position. Though an invalid claim, it is their only defense. Their assumption is that the phrase "that which is perfect" is a reference to the completed New Testament and that tongues were removed when the codex was complete.

I find great conflict in the belief that Scripture was written by "holy men of God [who] spoke as they were moved by the Holy Spirit" (2 Peter 1:21) but that when the Bible was "perfected"—or, completed—those "perfect" writings about prophecy, tongues and knowledge became imperfect. My question is this: How can the Bible qualify as being "that which is perfect" if it contains passages that are erroneous and unsafe for us to believe?

If this claim is so—that perfect Bible writings became imperfect when "that which is perfect [had] come"—we have a crisis that throws us completely out of authentic theology and into irrationality. The key is the word "then"—which is used three times in the text—and in all three instances referring to the same future date.

> But when that which is perfect has come, then that which is in part will be done away. . . . For now we see in a mirror, dimly, but then face to face. Now I know in part, but then I shall know just as I also am known.
>
> 1 Corinthians 13:10, 12

In all three instances where the word "then" appears, it points to the same future perfection. Have we come to the time when we no longer "see in a mirror, dimly," but "face to face"? Have we come to the time when we no longer know "in part" but "as I also am known"? No. Then we have not yet come to the time when "that which is perfect" has come. Thankfully, knowledge has not yet vanished away. There has been no diminishing of the provision of God.

The converted life cannot be begun or maintained except by the continual presence of the Holy Spirit. Religion can function without Him, but true spirituality cannot. It is He, the Holy Spirit, who hovered over the formless mass of the earth and brought order into its chaos and darkness. Indeed, from the beginning, the Holy Spirit is *identified with action*. Whether working in the vastness of the universe, or in the microscopic conception of a human life (and later in that human being's soul), it is the Holy Spirit whose ultimate goal is to bring us into comradeship with God. He will then sustain that union into eternal life. The Holy Spirit is God on the earth, the only source of life for the Church and the indispensable power for all the good that exists.

If we grieve the Holy Spirit He may become silent, imperceptible to us, and we will find ourselves seemingly abandoned to a frustrated and unspiritual state. David apparently feared this condition and cried out, "Take not Your Holy Spirit from me!"

The lives of scores of apathetic and unmotivated Christians attest to David's fear: It is possible to be born again and yet be in a spiritually lifeless condition. Such Christians and churches frequently resort to "religious" behavior to compensate for the loss of their true spirituality. Many never realize the tragedy of their loss. Saddest of all, a person who is not in submission to the Holy Spirit will eventually try to exercise power over the Holy Spirit.

### Your Inventory with the Holy Spirit

Consider that the Holy Spirit can be:

1. *Grieved:* "And do not grieve the Holy Spirit of God, by whom you were sealed for the day of redemption. Let all bitterness, wrath, anger, clamor, and evil speaking be put away from you, with all malice. And be kind to one another, tenderhearted, forgiving one another, even as God in Christ forgave you" (Ephesians 4:30–32).
2. *Resisted:* "You stiff-necked and uncircumcised in heart and ears! You always resist the Holy Spirit; as your fathers did, so do you" (Acts 7:51).
3. *Quenched:* "Do not quench the Spirit. Do not despise prophecies. Test all things; hold fast what is good. Abstain from every form of evil" (1 Thessalonians 5:19–22).
4. *Rebelled against:* "But they rebelled and grieved His Holy Spirit; so He turned Himself against them as an enemy, and He fought against them" (Isaiah 63:10).
5. *Rejected:* "Therefore, as the Holy Spirit says: 'Today, if you will hear His voice, do not harden your hearts as in the rebellion, in the day of trial in the wilderness, where your fathers tested Me, tried Me, and saw My works forty years'" (Hebrews 3:7–9).

**6. *Striven with:*** "And the LORD said, 'My Spirit shall not strive with man forever, for he is indeed flesh; yet his days shall be one hundred and twenty years'" (Genesis 6:3).

Meditate on these Scriptures prayerfully. Then ask the Holy Spirit to tell you the ways in which you have grieved, resisted, quenched, rebelled against, rejected and striven with Him. If you are sincere in your request, He will tell you. Listen carefully to His reply and absorb and study it. As in any case when you are seeking guidance and instruction, the internal answer you receive should be put to the test of Scripture. Command the "voice" speaking to you either to acknowledge that "Jesus Christ has come in the flesh" or to leave your thoughts altogether (1 John 4:2–3).

The Holy Spirit will not be insulted by your request. It is He who commanded the procedure as a safeguard against your being deceived. Do it! Examine your list carefully. Humble yourself before the Holy Spirit's rebuke and repent of your sin. If left unconfessed, any unrepented sin will insulate you from His companionship and obstruct the release of His power through you. It is too high a price to pay.

It is not the will of God that your ministry be powerless. Jesus proved this: "On the last day, that great day of the feast, Jesus stood and cried out, saying, 'If anyone thirsts, let him come to Me and drink. He who believes in Me, as the Scripture has said, out of his heart will flow rivers of living water.' But this He spoke concerning the Spirit, whom those believing in Him would receive; for the Holy Spirit was not yet given, because Jesus was not yet glorified" (John 7:37–39).

Jesus made this offer before Pentecost and in anticipation of the Spirit's outpouring. I understand this to mean that Pentecost's taking place on earth signaled the simultaneous glorifying of Jesus in heaven. The coronation was above, the celebration was below. Jesus' offer of the Holy Spirit is your personal invitation to receive the anointing and the power. Get it!

The modern Church lacks miraculous power because it has wrongly assumed that preaching the Gospel requires nothing more than the presentation of Bible facts. *This is absolutely not so!* Seminaries and Bible schools, as wonderful as they are, can only impart academic knowledge. Even those that acknowledge the need for spiritual gifts are powerless to provide them. These giftings come directly from Jesus as the baptizer in the Holy Spirit—or we do not get them at all (John 1:33). A pastor can have numerous university degrees on his office wall and yet still may be disqualified from providing genuine New Testament ministry.

The book of Acts gives us a working model of a conscientious, godly pastor who had excellent credentials for ministry but who preached a weak, ineffective Gospel: Apollos. This man served a small, struggling congregation in the city of Ephesus. Acts explains that Apollos was a Jewish convert, an eloquent man, mighty in Scripture, instructed in the way of the Lord and fervent in spirit, who taught accurately the things of the Lord but knew only the "baptism of John." Simply put, Apollos knew nothing about the baptism in the Spirit, the anointing and the spiritual gifts.

He was ignorant because he had never been taught—not because he had knowingly rejected the truth. In our day, pastors generally fall into two groups: (1) those who have never been taught and are innocently ignorant of spiritual empowering, and (2) those who willfully reject spiritual power and the gifts. For nearly thirty years I belonged to the latter group who knowingly rejected vital parts of Scripture.

While Apollos was away, Paul visited this church of twelve male disciples and immediately recognized their spiritual powerlessness. He asked them, "Did you receive the Holy Spirit when you believed?" They responded, "We have not so much as heard whether there is a Holy Spirit" (Acts 19:2). Paul then taught them about the Holy Spirit's empowering, and when he "laid hands on them, the Holy Spirit came upon them, and they spoke with tongues and prophesied" (verse 6).

That event proved to be a cataclysmic change not only for Ephesus but for the entire Roman world. Under Apollos' ministry, the church at Ephesus had accomplished nothing to awaken the city. It demonstrated no Kingdom power, remained spiritually paralyzed, and except for the local synagogue its presence was virtually unknown. In this spiritual state, the congregation had no effective witness, made no impact on the people and was no threat to "powers, principalities, rulers of the darkness of this world." Instead, a dark cloud of paganism gripped the land with unchallenged control. The Temple of Diana (or Artemis), already famous as the greatest of all the Seven Wonders of the Ancient World, dominated the area. Then Ephesus experienced a "Kingdom of God" earthquake. Paul was not the power behind it, but he was the instrument for the truth that produced the shaking.

Much of modern, evangelical Christianity parallels the ministry of Apollos. It is sincere and eloquent, accurately teaching Bible truth as far as it allows itself to believe. But its doctrine is measured by its own opinion, for it is afraid to measure its doctrine by Scripture. Traditional Christianity is dominated by the doctrine of dispensationalism, which claims the miraculous gifts of the Holy Spirit have passed away. Yet Jesus said no such change would occur: "All authority has been given to Me in heaven and on earth. Go therefore and make disciples of all the nations, baptizing them in the name of the Father and of the Son and of the Holy Spirit, teaching them to observe all things that I have commanded you; and lo, I am with you always, even to the end of the age" (Matthew 28:18–20). Jesus fully expected the Church "at the end of the age" to believe and teach "all things" that He had commanded the original disciples.

## The Release of Power through the Death of Ego

For years, I correctly preached that the rending of the Temple veil at Jesus' death forever ended God's acceptance of animal sacrifice. One day, however, as I was studying the passage, the Holy Spirit stopped me and said, "Read it again." I did so. It was not until the fourth or fifth reading that a new truth dawned on me about the veil. The best way I can describe the Holy Spirit's message is as follows:

He said, "You are thinking only of the blood going *into* the holy of holies. With the veil rent and the Temple opened, what is now free to come *out* of the holy of holies?"

I was awestruck. I knew the shekinah glory was the only light in the holy of holies. That light was the Holy Spirit Himself. With the veil torn (in terms of typology), there was no longer an obstruction to keep the shekinah from flashing outward to the rest of the Temple.

In that moment, I saw two astonishing, parallel truths: In an identical way, the Holy Spirit flooded out of heaven's temple into the Upper Room at Pentecost—and the Holy Spirit flooded out of a believer's temple-body to heal or bless, just as a prisoner had once done with me (Acts 2:1–4; John 7:38).

The Spirit's lesson continued: "Charles, your temple-body is flesh, soul, spirit. It corresponds to the outer court, holy place and holy of holies. Your hands are an extension of that temple. With your veil torn, I am free to move to your outer court and upon the person on whom you lay hands. At the time of your wife's wreck, you went through a death—but in that death you finally committed your life 'into My hands.' That is when your veil was torn."

The months that followed were revelatory. In part, I saw the beauty of "dying in Christ" as I had never seen it before. This death is not sacrificial and foreboding. It is a matter, rather, of God wanting us to surrender our depraved self-will to His perfect will. When I finally emerged in 1977 from that long, dark storm, submitted to God and became better informed scripturally, I was a new man—with a new message and anointing for new ministry. Today, at age eighty-plus, my health is stronger and my ministry more relevant, more powerful and more far-reaching than in all previous years combined—and the end is not in sight.

I urge you: Come go with me! Say with Paul, "I have been crucified with Christ: it is no longer I who live, but Christ lives in me; and the life which I now live in the flesh I live by faith in the Son of God, who loved me and gave himself for me" (Galatians 2:20).

How does one receive the anointing? Jesus said, "Your heavenly Father [will] give the Holy Spirit to those who ask Him!" (Luke 11:13). Ask, friend, ask! If you have not done so, stop your foolish arguing and receive it. Your Christian walk will be transformed.

# eleven

# Receiving the Power

"If anyone thirsts let him come to me and drink. He who believes in Me, as the Scripture has said, out of his heart will flow rivers of living water." But this He spoke concerning the Spirit, whom those believing in Him would receive.

John 7:37–39

Most preachers would make good martyrs; they are so dry they would burn well.

Charles Spurgeon

I have been in ordained ministry more than sixty years. I want to give as freely to you as the Holy Spirit has given to me. My call, concern and mission are to help you minister in the anointed fullness and power of the Holy Spirit—so that your church may experience an invasive, explosive, all-empowering, permanent anointing of the Holy Spirit.

I want it said of you, me and the Church what Jesus said of Himself: "The Spirit of the LORD is upon Me, because He has

191

anointed Me to preach the gospel to the poor; He has sent Me to heal the brokenhearted, to proclaim liberty to the captives and recovery of sight to the blind, to set at liberty those who are oppressed; to proclaim the acceptable year of the LORD" (Luke 4:18–19).

On the final day of the Feast of Tabernacles, Jesus made the most astounding offer humankind has ever heard: "If anyone thirsts let him come unto Me and drink." Those who drank would receive the Holy Spirit. The same creative Spirit who brought life and light into the chaotic mass of the earth in the beginning was now presented as a gift to humankind. Millions have received it.

In a more private way, when Jesus conferred Kingdom rule upon the apostles, He called "His twelve disciples together and gave them power and authority over all demons, and to cure diseases" (Luke 9:1). Their baptism in the Holy Spirit would come later. Anticipating that event, Jesus gave them the privilege to minister with Him.

The key word here is "together." Jesus did not find John at the Jordan, Matthew at the Mediterranean and Peter at Galilee and confer power upon them separately. *He called them together.* So it was then, and so it is now. Those who wish to minister in the anointing of the Holy Spirit must be willing to accept "togetherness" in the whole Body of Christ. There is but one anointing provided for the Church in all ages (Acts 2). We may continue functioning within a specific denomination, but we cannot reject the rest of the Body. We must operate in the whole or not at all. God does not read church signs, nor may you and I.

The gift of the Spirit is a Kingdom endowment. It is *not* a provision of the Church and can never be limited by the Church. Those who try to limit the work of the Spirit to their denominational box are reviling Him. Jesus explained this when He said, "But if I cast out demons by the Spirit of God, surely the kingdom of God has come upon you" (Matthew 12:28). The Church has no such power of its own.

If you have not experienced the baptism in the Spirit, you may easily do so. With right preparation, every sincere believer can receive the Spirit's gift. In that baptism, the impartation of spiritual gifts and power is automatic (1 Corinthians 12–14).

My recommendation is that you find a body of anointed believers who understand your need, that you participate in their worship and that you have some reliable person lay hands on you. Do not allow suspicious persons to minister to you. Know them well. The one doing so should pray for the impartation in Jesus' name.

If no such group is available, then devote uninterrupted time to private worship, present yourself to the Lord and ask Him to fill you. In that solitary setting, you can still receive. Believe what Jesus said: "For everyone who asks receives" (Matthew 7:8). "If you then, being evil, know how to give good gifts to your children, how much more will your heavenly Father give the Holy Spirit to those who ask Him!" (Luke 11:13).

Remember that God deals with each person individually. I received the baptism as a tidal wave crashing down on me, top to bottom. My wife received it as a tide coming in and quietly filling her from bottom to top. I did not speak in tongues immediately. She did. But we both received phenomenally. So will you.

Once you have received the baptism, you must protect it as you would a treasured jewel. While the "gifts and calling of God are without turning back," the anointing will cease to function if the Holy Spirit becomes grieved. When you fail, God understands your weaknesses better than you and will be loving and patient as you mature. Your noblest and most difficult task is to pursue a state of grace in which your conformity to Christ becomes the great concern of life.

The effort to pursue this state of grace becomes complicated only when we try to achieve it in our own strength. It is astonishingly easy when we allow the Holy Spirit to accomplish it through us. If you are a pastor or in some form of public service, be aware that ministering in the power should be effortless. You are a vessel through whom His power passes—the wire, not the electricity. At whatever point you begin "trying" to do the works of the Spirit, you are out of the will of God. Human efforts, emotion and hype grieve the Spirit. Ministering in His power is never a "soul" effort. Your biggest task is to "hear what the Spirit is saying" and obey. Leave the work to Him.

In hands-on ministry, people sometimes get shoved to the floor by exuberant ministers. This is an insult to the Holy Spirit and creates a pseudo-experience for the one seeking to receive. In such moments, human ego becomes a hazard. If the one doing the ministry is truly anointed, such action is totally unnecessary.

I am frequently in meetings where the Holy Spirit moves powerfully and in great demonstration (1 Corinthians 2:4). People are miraculously healed, delivered from demons, filled with the Spirit and physically overcome in spectacular ways. "Signs and wonders" occur spontaneously. People suffering from clinical depression have unexpectedly laughed their way to normalcy. Many vibrate uncontrollably from the Holy Spirit's electricity-like supercharge.

My task is to stay out of God's way and let the miraculous happen. Lives are radically changed in a second's time when the Holy Spirit invades the scene.

### God's Sense of Humor

At a meeting in Florida, the Holy Spirit was moving visibly and scores of people were experiencing the power of God in life-changing ways.

A woman who owned several estates, yachts, racehorses, Rolls Royces, a private jet, big diamonds and an apartment at the Waldorf Astoria Hotel in New York came to a meeting. When I laid hands on her she was slammed to the floor so fast that her blond wig flew off and landed about three feet beyond her in the aisle. She never knew it happened. The Holy Spirit swept her into such a powerful embrace with Himself that she lay there basking in the glory. An usher replaced the wig. Such is the humor of God! Was she blessed? Yes, her life changed dramatically.

Sometimes, without explanation, the anointing will lift from meetings. The power will be gone and the manifestations will stop abruptly. When that happens, I can usually point to a single reason: The congregation has quit worshiping. When the Body loses its corporate unity with the Spirit and believers revert to their individual concerns, the power fades. Worship is the uniting factor for a congregation—and for an individual. A life that does not connect to God profoundly in worship will rarely connect to Him in the invasion of the Holy Spirit.

Earlier, I observed that getting the power in us is not as great a problem as getting the power to come out of us (Acts 1:8). Failure results when carnal factors insulate us and prevent the power's outflow. This fact is illustrated in Luke 9, where six reasons for the disciples' failure are identified. The Bible preserves these for us in careful detail.

Jesus "called His twelve disciples together and gave them power and authority over all demons, and to cure diseases" (Luke 9:1). He then left nine of them at the bottom of the mountain while He, Peter, James and John went to the top:

> Now it came to pass, about eight days after these sayings, that He took Peter, John, and James and went up the mountain to pray. As He prayed, the appearance of His face was altered, and His robe became white and glistening. And behold, two men talked with Him, who were Moses and Elijah, who appeared in glory and spoke of His decease which He was about to accomplish at Jerusalem.
>
> Luke 9:28–31

## Reasons for Failure

In Jesus' absence, a distraught father brought his demonized son to the disciples at the base of the mountain. Even though

195

Jesus had just given His disciples power, they failed to cast out the spirit (9:37–40).

> Now it happened on the next day, when they had come down from the mountain, that a great multitude met Him. Suddenly a man from the multitude cried out, saying, "Teacher, I implore You, look on my son, for he is my only child. And behold, a spirit seizes him, and he suddenly cries out; it convulses him so that he foams at the mouth; and it departs from him with great difficulty, bruising him. So I implored Your disciples to cast it out, but they could not."

Luke gives six detailed reasons for the disciples' failure. As you read, inspect your own heart and life prayerfully:

1. *The disciples' lack of faith and their un-repented perversity.* "Then Jesus answered and said, 'O faithless and perverse generation, how long shall I be with you and bear with you? Bring your son here.' And as he was still coming, the demon threw him down and convulsed him. Then Jesus rebuked the unclean spirit, healed the child, and gave him back to his father. And they were all amazed at the majesty of God" (9:41–43).
2. *Ego—the disciples' fear of showing their ignorance.* "But while everyone marveled at all the things which Jesus did, He said to His disciples, 'Let these words sink down into your ears, for the Son of Man is about to be betrayed into the hands of men.' But they did not understand this saying, and it was hidden from them so that they did not perceive it; and they were afraid to ask Him about this saying" (verses 43–45).
3. *Pride.* "Then a dispute arose among them as to which of them would be greatest" (verse 46).
4. *Sectarianism.* "Now John answered and said, 'Master, we saw someone casting out demons in Your name, and we forbade him because he does not follow with us.' But

Jesus said to him, 'Do not forbid him, for he who is not against us is on our side'" (verses 49–50).

5. *Unforgiveness and desire for revenge.* "And as they went, they entered a village of the Samaritans, to prepare for Him. But they did not receive Him, because His face was *set* for the journey to Jerusalem. And when His disciples James and John saw this, they said, 'Lord, do You want us to command fire to come down from heaven and consume them, just as Elijah did?'" (verses 52–54).

6. *Refusal to acknowledge unclean spirits in themselves.* "But He turned and rebuked them, and said, 'You do not know what manner of spirit you are of. For the Son of Man did not come to destroy men's lives but to save them' And they went to another village" (verses 55–56).

While there are other reasons the disciples failed, these six are stark reminders of our own potential to misuse holy opportunities.

### Victims of Hardness of Heart

Without recognizing the tragic condition in themselves, the disciples allowed "hardness of heart" to paralyze their spiritual growth and bring failure to their ministries. If the hardened-heart problem was very real for the first-century believers, what about us? As I observe the broad spectrum of ministers today, I am convinced we are in much greater danger of hardness of heart than of moral failure. Both are tragic destroyers.

When the disciples became fearful over the lack of food, Jesus said to them:

"Why do you reason because you have no bread? Do you not yet perceive nor understand? Is your heart still hardened? Having eyes, do you not see? And having ears, do you not hear? And do you not remember? When I broke the five loaves for the five

197

thousand, how many baskets full of fragments did you take up?" They said to Him, "Twelve." "Also, when I broke the seven for the four thousand, how many large baskets full of fragments did you take up?" And they said, "Seven." So He said to them, "How is it you do not understand?"

Mark 8:17–21

The disciples did not realize that the spiritual world in which Jesus lived and worked overrode food deficiencies and all other needs in their physical world. This was clear when they saw Jesus walking on the water toward their boat in the midst of a storm:

They supposed it was a ghost, and cried out; for they all saw Him and were troubled. But immediately He talked with them and said to them, "Be of good cheer! It is I; do not be afraid." Then He went up into the boat to them, and the wind ceased. And they were greatly amazed in themselves beyond measure, and marveled. For they had not understood about the loaves, because their heart was hardened.

Mark 6:49–52

The disciples could have seen these truths much sooner but did not because, Scripture says, their hearts were hardened. Likewise today, Christians who close their eyes to Scripture, blindly defend denominational bias and oppose the Spirit's baptismal work should be aware of this solemn danger. The Bible has as many warnings for the saint as it does for the sinner. Here is another warning addressed specifically to the believer:

Therefore, as the Holy Spirit says: "Today, if you will hear His voice, do not harden your hearts as in the rebellion, in the day of trial in the wilderness, where your fathers tested Me, tried Me, and saw My works forty years. Therefore I was angry with that generation, and said, 'They always go astray in their heart, and they have not known My ways.' So I swore in My wrath, 'They shall not enter My rest.'" Beware, brethren, lest there be in any of you an evil heart of unbelief in departing from the living God; but exhort one another daily, while it is called "Today," lest any of you be hardened through the deceitfulness of sin. For we have become partakers of Christ if we hold the beginning of our confidence steadfast to the end, while it is said: "Today, if you will hear His voice, do not harden your hearts as in the rebellion."

Hebrews 3:7–15

## Some Factors That Cause Hardness

What factors cause such hardness in dedicated believers? Here are a few:

- disappointments in church life, personal life, family, health
- attitudes of rejection, suspicion, anger, jealousy
- believing God has dealt with us unfairly, ignored vital prayer requests
- seeing ourselves as failures, poor performers, incapable of success, having no value
- thinking that life will end for us with dreams and hopes unfulfilled
- other false concepts retained from childhood, often marked by abuse

These circumstances can produce a common effect in a believer: *hardness of heart.*

I repeat from the previous chapter: There can be no converted life begun or maintained except by the continual presence of the Holy Spirit. Religion can function without Him, but true spiritual life cannot. From the beginning of the Bible record, the Holy Spirit is identified with *action.* It is impossible for the Holy Spirit to work in a church or ministry and for that body to remain lifeless and unmotivated. The Spirit's very nature prohibits every circumstance of inertia.

199

"Now the Lord is the Spirit; and where the Spirit of the Lord is, there is liberty" (2 Corinthians 3:17). The presence of this liberty assures life, vitality, action. The Holy Spirit is never responsible for religious bondage. We can be assured that if it is present, He is not.

## A Good Man Who Failed

Earlier, I mentioned the church in Ephesus that Apollos served as pastor (Acts 18:24–28). Scripture outlines six qualities about this church and its leader. This passage may also describe your ministry. If so, accept the rebuke, surrender your ego and make the necessary change.

1. Apollos was an eloquent man.
2. He was mighty in Scripture.
3. He was instructed in the way of the Lord.
4. He was fervent in spirit.
5. He taught accurately the things of the Lord.
6. He knew only the "baptism of John"—nothing about the baptism in the Spirit.

These same features identify many great preachers in our day. In spite of Apollos' qualifications, his ministry was virtually a failure because he had not received the Holy Spirit's power. When the apostle Paul visited the church at Ephesus, he provided the window through which the Spirit's power roared. Other windows, including that of Apollos, were already present in Ephesus, but *they had never been opened.*

Compare your ministry to that of Apollos. Is your window open or closed? Are you operating in the power of the Holy Spirit? If not, why not? You need not remain like Apollos. In spite of paganism's dark and ominous presence in Ephesus, Paul's first mission in the city was not to attack it. His first mission was to impart the power of the Holy Spirit to the Church.

In the identical fashion that Ananias earlier laid hands on Paul in Damascus "that [he might] receive [his] sight and be filled with the Holy Spirit" (Acts 9:17), Paul laid hands on the Ephesian believers, with the same hell-shattering results. After "the Holy Spirit came upon them," the power of the Gospel blew the city of Ephesus apart (Acts 19:6).

Those Ephesian believers—there were twelve of them—became spiritual Herculeses who multiplied into a hundred, then five thousand, then tens of thousands. Thousands more were converted, the Church exploded in power, the Temple of Diana was ultimately emptied and destroyed and the city of Ephesus changed into a Christian citadel known throughout the Roman world. Within two years Paul was gone, but for centuries the fire of the Ephesian revival blazed out of control.

What caused such a revolutionary transformation? It was not Paul. Hear me carefully: It was the power of the Holy Spirit working *through* Paul. Apollos lacked the power because he and his little congregation knew nothing about the Holy Spirit's baptism and gifts. In spite of this pastor's other qualifications, his ministry remained impotent. Be aware of this important point of theology: The power working in Paul did not come to him on the Damascus Road when he met Jesus—not at all. It came in the Damascus room, under the hands of Ananias, when Paul was filled with the Holy Spirit (Acts 9:17). Meeting Jesus saved Paul for heaven. Meeting the Holy Spirit empowered him for Kingdom ministry. This was in perfect accord with the experience of the first disciples.

On the day of His resurrection, Jesus appeared in the closed room where the disciples were assembled, breathed on them and said, "Receive the Holy Spirit" (John 20:22). I understand this to be the day they received the New Covenant birth. Jesus then instructed them to wait in the city of Jerusalem until they were "baptized with the Holy Spirit," saying, "You shall receive power when the Holy Spirit has come upon you" (Acts 1:8). This was the empowering they received at Pentecost—empowering for ministry.

Identically, the believers in Ephesus were already born again when Paul arrived. They had had a "Damascus Road" encounter with Jesus. But not until Paul appeared and laid hands on them did they experience their "Damascus room" baptism in the Holy Spirit. That event anointed them with Kingdom power—and from that moment on, Ephesian paganism was doomed. One destiny awaited it: It would bow its knee to the Lordship of Jesus Christ.

Is it possible that a man as qualified for ministry as Apollos could *still* lack the most essential factor of all—the empowering of the Holy Spirit? Yes. It is just as likely that you—mighty as Apollos—could still have an impotent church, an ineffective ministry, failed and fruitless efforts, in spite of your training and ability. Thousands of congregations today, taught by modern-day Apolloses, are cowering under the shadow of Diana. If these churches had the empowering of the Holy Spirit, it would never be.

It matters not how eloquent you are, how mighty in the Scripture, how instructed in the ways of the Lord, how accurately you teach the things of God, how fervent you may be in spirit or how many degrees hang on your office wall—you are still spinning your theological wheels, accomplishing minimal results, until you have been filled with the Holy Spirit. That is not my word—it is God's word. If it were true of Apollos and the Ephesians, I guarantee it can be equally true of you or anyone else today. You need the Holy Spirit. You need His power. If you fail to get it, the fault is not God's. He has freely provided it for you.

Your life, your home, your work, your ministry, can be transformed. No matter who you are, you can receive more of heaven's inexhaustible supply. Jesus is the Baptizer in the Holy Spirit. Drop your opposition and receive all He has. The Word, the Spirit and the Power are yours. Here is my concluding prayer for you:

God Almighty! We pray Your Kingdom come, Your will be done, in the life of the one now reading this book. Holy Spirit, cause this one's heart to cry out for more of Your anointing, Your glory, Your power. Show this one that receiving You is as simple as drinking the water Jesus offered. Let him go with Jesus to the Jordan. This very moment, let him disappear beneath the water and rise again to behold the Dove of the Holy Spirit coming upon him.

Let this be your response:

> Great Baptizer, I am coming
> Yielding heart and soul to Thee,
> Plunge me in the Spirit's fullness,
> Baptize in the cloud and sea.
> Wash, anoint me, fill, empower!
> Above the waters let me rise,
> Singing in new tongues of angels
> Change my earth to Paradise!
> Amen!

# Conclusion

## R. T. Kendall

You have now been exposed to the message that Jack, Charles and I have preached for the past several years. I hope that what we have said has stirred your heart and has been a blessing to you. We regard it as a most high privilege to preach this message wherever we go and to speak to you as we have in this book.

We now want to end with both a caution and a hope.

First, the caution. I have been a student of Church history in general and revival in particular for most of my life. Among other things I have learned is that God has been pleased to show Himself in a variety of ways over the centuries. God used Tertullian (c. 160–c. 225) wonderfully in his day. What God did through Athanasius (c. 296–373) and Augustine (354–430) was crucial and pivotal for the Church. What God did through the Great Reformation with men like Martin Luther (1483–1546) and John Calvin (1509–1564) was truly revival. What happened through the ministries of Jonathan Edwards (1703–1758), George Whitefield (1714–1770) and John Wesley (1703–1791) resulted in a great and powerful awakening on both sides of the Atlantic. The Cane Ridge Revival—often called "America's Second Great Awakening" in the early nineteenth century—is partly what gave America her Bible Belt.

Later in the same century, however, there emerged a mixed blessing in the ministry of Charles G. Finney (1792–1875). There is little doubt that Finney saw a mighty work of God in his day. It seems to me, however, there is a sad side of his legacy—namely, his fostering the idea that "if we do our part, God will do His part." Finney gave the impression that if the Church will do certain things—e.g., pray and fast over a period of time—revival will surely come. Subsequent Church history has proved him wrong. Many people have tried this "formula" without success.

My point is this. We want to conclude our book with this caution: namely, that you, the reader, will *not* regard what you have read in the preceding pages as a "formula" for the revival we desperately need. It is not that. The fact that we have sought to bring the Word and Spirit together so that it may produce power is no guarantee that power will inevitably follow. God is sovereign. He said to Moses, "I will have mercy on whom I will have mercy" (Exodus 33:19, NIV), and this refers equally to any prayer for revival. There is nothing you and I can do to twist God's arm to make Him pour out His Holy Spirit in power.

Indeed, my own 25 years at Westminster Chapel did not witness the revival we prayed for, although I did all that I knew to do to bring the Word and Spirit together. We became more evangelistic than ever. I opened the door to the prophetic ministry. I accepted a certain movement of the Spirit that many felt was not of God. I brought Jack and Charles to Westminster. Along the way we used to hear suggestions as to what we might further do to make things "happen." I will never forget an anonymous letter written to me saying there was *one* reason revival had not come to Westminster Chapel: The ladies (including my wife, Louise) were not wearing hats. Another suggestion was that our ecclesiology was not sound. Another had to do with the frequency with which we should observe the Lord's Supper. I could go on and on.

I am saying, then, that at the end of the day we all must rest on the sovereignty of God to bring the outpouring of the Holy

Spirit that is needed in our time. As for my hope that "Isaac is coming"—which I believe with all my heart—only God can bring this about, and no "formula" is going to hasten it.

What Jack, Charles and I have sought hard to do is to be utterly biblical. I have sought faithfully to uphold the Gospel. Jack has spent the whole of his life trying to make room for the Holy Spirit in his ministry. Charles, who came from a hyper-Calvinistic background, has seen extraordinary things in his own life and ministry. The three of us together have traveled far and wide with the message that the Word and the Spirit must come together.

We close this book, secondly and finally, with hope—and it is a thrilling hope indeed. I believe with all my heart that what we have pointed to in this book is *going to happen*—and that it is not far away. The Word and the Spirit *will* come together before Jesus comes again. Whether the three of us see this in our lifetime is one thing—but it is coming. The three of us have an assured *hope* that the greatest work of the Spirit since Pentecost is truly on the way. We acknowledge, indeed, that only God can make this happen.

Yet we equally believe in crying out to God day and night with all our hearts until He does show up in the kind of power this book has emphasized. I lean on the parable of the persistent widow in Luke 18:1–8. Jesus plainly told us to be like this persistent widow—to pray and not give up. We are on solid biblical ground, therefore, to plead before our heavenly Father for Him to step in during these perilous times in which we live. In a word: We must pray more than ever, intercede more than ever, stand in the gap more than ever—and do so believing we are being heard and that God will therefore answer our prayer. In other words, *we believe that what we have taught in this book is at hand.*

We pray, then, that what we have written will stir up godly men and women to seek the Lord more than ever, to preach the Gospel more than ever, and to be open to the Holy Spirit's immediate and direct witness more than ever. Jack, Charles and I pray for you, the reader, that God the Father, Son and Holy Spirit will be upon you with more grace than ever—now and evermore. Amen.

R. T. Kendall is a graduate of Southern Baptist Theological Seminary and Oxford University (D.Phil.). A protégé of Dr. Martyn Lloyd-Jones of the historic Westminster Chapel in London, R. T. himself served as senior minister there for 25 years. He is the author of numerous bestselling books, including *Total Forgiveness*, *God Meant It for Good* and *Did You Think to Pray?* He conducts conferences all over the world and spends his time preaching and writing, including a bimonthly column for *Ministry Today*. He and his wife, Louise, live on Hickory Lake in Hendersonville, Tennessee, where he fishes occasionally.

Jack Taylor is president of Dimensions Ministries, is the author of thirteen books and has a ministry that has spanned six decades. Jack graduated from Baptist Theological Seminary, has pastored several churches and has witnessed spiritual awakenings in the local church. He travels extensively, declaring the promises of God for revival. His heart is in the Kingdom of God, and he believes that true revival in the Church awaits a rediscovery of the Kingdom. God has gifted Jack with an apostolic insight into the Word of God and the heart to communicate the fullness of God's Kingdom. He and his wife, Friede, reside in Melbourne, Florida.

Charles Carrin's years in ministry span sixty years, most of which time his beliefs and practices denied the supernatural works and gifts of the Holy Spirit. A crisis time in his own life, however, caused him to revise his theology. Today his ministry is characterized by displays of the power of God in salvation as well as deliverance and healing. Charles has since traveled to many parts of the world teaching others how to receive and minister in the empowering of the Holy Spirit. He studied at the University of Georgia and Columbia Theological Summary and holds an honorary doctor of divinity degree from the Evangelical Bible College and Seminary. He lives in Boynton Beach, Florida.